JUSTICE IN AFRICA

Contemporary Perspectives on Developing Societies

JOHN MUKUM MBAKU, Series General Editor, Weber State University
MWANGI S. KIMENYI, Series Associate Editor, The University of Connecticut

Between 1989 and 1991, there were several changes in the global political economy that have had significant impact on policy reform in developing societies. The most important of these were the collapse of socialism in Eastern Europe, the subsequent disintegration of the Soviet Union, the cessation of superpower rivalry, and the demise of apartheid in South Africa. These events have provided scholars a new and challenging research agenda: To help the peoples of the Third World participate more effectively in the new global economy. Given existing conditions in these societies, the first line of business for researchers would be to help these countries establish and maintain transparent, accountable and participatory governance structures and, at the same time, provide themselves with more viable economic infrastructures. The Contemporary Perspectives on Developing Societies series was founded to serve as an outlet for such policy relevant research. It is expected that books published in this series will provide rigorous analyses of issues relevant to the peoples of the Third World and their efforts to improve their participation in the global economy.

Also in the series

Hope, K.R., Sr. (ed.) (1997), *Structural Adjustment, Reconstruction and Development in Africa*.
Mbaku, J. M. and Ihonvbere, J.O. (eds.) (1998), *Multiparty Democracy and Political Change: Constraints to Democratization in Africa*.
Kimenyi, M.S., Wieland, R.C. and Von Pischke, J.D. (eds.) (1998), *Strategic Issues in Microfinance*.
Magnarella, P.J. (ed.) (1999), *Middle East and North Africa: Governance, Democratization, Human Rights*.
Mbaku, J.M. (ed.) (1999), *Preparing Africa for the Twenty-First Century: Strategies for Peaceful Coexistence and Sustainable Development*.

Justice in Africa
Rwanda's Genocide, Its Courts, and the UN Criminal Tribunal

PAUL J. MAGNARELLA
University of Florida
Gainesville, Florida, USA

LONDON AND NEW YORK

First published 2000 by Ashgate Publishing

Reissued 2018 by Routledge
2 Park Square, Milton Park, Abingdon, Oxon OX14 4RN
711 Third Avenue, New York, NY 10017, USA

Routledge is an imprint of the Taylor & Francis Group, an informa business

Copyright © Paul J. Magnarella 2000

All rights reserved. No part of this book may be reprinted or reproduced or utilised in any form or by any electronic, mechanical, or other means, now known or hereafter invented, including photocopying and recording, or in any information storage or retrieval system, without permission in writing from the publishers.

Notice:
Product or corporate names may be trademarks or registered trademarks, and are used only for identification and explanation without intent to infringe.

Publisher's Note
The publisher has gone to great lengths to ensure the quality of this reprint but points out that some imperfections in the original copies may be apparent.

Disclaimer
The publisher has made every effort to trace copyright holders and welcomes correspondence from those they have been unable to contact.

A Library of Congress record exists under LC control number: 99076655

ISBN 13: 978-1-138-70102-1 (hbk)
ISBN 13: 978-1-138-70101-4 (pbk)
ISBN 13: 978-1-315-20429-1 (ebk)

Contents

About the Author	vii
Map	ix
Preface	xi
1. Comprehending the Rwandan Genocide	1
2. The International Role	29
3. Expanding the Frontiers of Humanitarian Law: The International Tribunal for Rwanda	41
4. Criticism and Controversy	59
5. The Situation in Rwanda	71
6. The Kambanda Case	85
7. The Akayesu Case	95
8. Conclusion	111
Appendix A. United Nations Security Council Resolution 955 with the Statute of the International Tribunal for Rwanda Annexed	115
Appendix B. Amendments to the Statute of the International Tribunal for Rwanda	131
Appendix C. Indictment of Jean Paul Akayesu	135
Bibliography	143
Index	151

About the Author

PAUL J. MAGNARELLA, (Ph.D. Cultural Anthropology, Harvard University; J.D. International Law, University of Florida) is Professor of Anthropology and Affiliated Professor of Law and African Studies at the University of Florida. He has served as an Expert on Mission with the United Nations International Criminal Tribunal for the Former Yugoslavia and as President of the Association of Third World Studies. He currently serves as that Association's Special Counsel and Representative to the United Nations. His previous books include: *The Peasant Venture* (1979), *Tradition and Change in a Turkish Town* (1981), *Human Materialism: A Model of Sociocultural Systems and a Strategy for Analysis* (1993), and *Anatolia's Loom: Studies in Turkish Culture, Society, Politics and Law* (1998). He has also edited *The Middle East and North Africa: Democratization, Governance, and Human Rights* (1999) and special issues of *Third World Studies*, *The African Studies Quarterly*, *Human Peace and Human Rights*, *The International Journal of Anthropology*, and *Global Bioethics*.

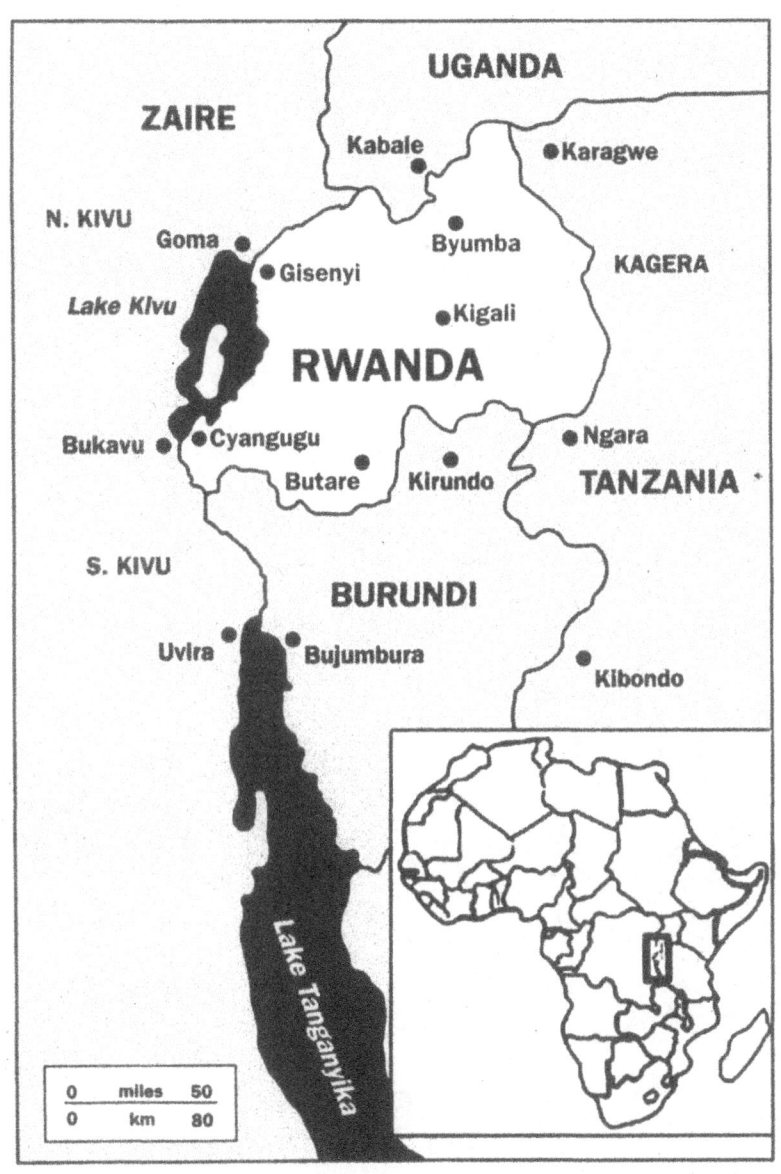

Rwanda

Preface

This book deals with the Rwandan genocide and judicial responses to it both at the national level of Rwandan courts and at the international level of the United Nations war crimes tribunal. I have written it for readers who are not necessarily legal specialists or anthropologists, but who want to understand why this horrendous human tragedy occurred and what, in the name of law and justice, is being done about it. Consequently, I have avoided technical vocabulary and extensive footnoting. I begin the book with an anthropological analysis of the genocide and its causes, utilizing the human materialist paradigm. I present elements from Rwanda's history that seem to have contributed significantly to the calamity of 1994. Chapter 2 discusses the roles played by certain foreign countries and the United Nations immediately before and during the genocide. Chapter 3 describes the creation, structure, and operations of the United Nations International Criminal Tribunal for Rwanda, while Chapter 4 deals with some of the criticisms and controversies surrounding it. Rwanda's own judicial responses to genocide–its large prison population, 'genocide law' and special genocide courts–are dealt with in Chapter 5. Chapters 6 and 7 discuss the Tribunal's first two cases, both of which are significant for the history of Rwanda and the development of international humanitarian law. The book does not deal with many related issues of importance to post-genocide Rwanda, such as the refugee problems in neighboring countries or the political and humanitarian crises in Zaire (Democratic Republic of the Congo).

Writing this book was greatly facilitated by my two visits to the Rwandan Tribunal in Arusha, Tanzania, in the spring of 1997 and then 1998, during which times I observed on-going trials, talked with members of the Tribunal and the press, and collected Tribunal documents. My research at the Tribunal was made most pleasant and productive because of the kind help of many people there. Among those who were willing to talk and share ideas with me were Tribunal attorneys Fred Harhoff, Kingsley Chiedu Mohalu, and Alessandro Caldarone and defense attorney Tiphaine Dickson. Bocar Sy and Pauline W. Ndiritu of the Press and Public Affairs Office were most helpful, as were newspeople Thierry Cruvellier of Intermedia and Premy Kibanga of East

African News. I also appreciated John Mashaka's warm greeting whenever I entered the courtroom gallery.

My interest in Rwanda and the Rwandan Tribunal was stimulated by my 1995 experience working as a pro bono expert on mission with the UN International Criminal Tribunal for the Former Yugoslavia (ICTY), located at The Hague, The Netherlands. Many of the people there contributed directly and indirectly to my understanding of humanitarian law and the two UN ad hoc tribunals. They include, but are not limited to: ICTY President Antonio Cassese, whose intellect I admire and whose generosity I will never forget; Registrar Dorothee de Sampayo Garrido-Nijgh, who received me graciously; Deputy Registrar Dominique Marro; Christian Chartier, Valerie Brion, and Randa Alatas of the Press and Information Office; staff members Isabelle Lambert, Carmela Javier, Roland Alders, and Edgar van Dijk; legal assistants Niccolo Figa-Talamanca, Elizabeth Anderson, James Sloan, John Jones, Faiza King, and Rafaelle Maison; senior legal officer Fernando Castanon; and prosecutor Greg Kehoe. I apologize to others whose names I have inadvertently omitted.

I also want to thank those special people who made my life most pleasant and comfortable during my stays in The Netherlands and Tanzania. At The Hague, they were Alexandra and Franz Tuininga and their wonderful family. In the Arusha area they were Pete and Charlotte O'Neal. I could not have been more fortunate in meeting them. Fate blessed me with their hospitality and friendship. They have become my dear brothers and sisters.

Thanks go to my family for putting up with my absences abroad and paper clutter at home. As usual, my wife Sharlene was a patient proof-reader. I am most grateful to Margaret Joyner for her fine editorial and formatting work, to Mary 'Sam' Allen for producing the map of Rwanda, and to Kamal Ferali for assisting me with French. Work at both tribunals was made possible by the financial help of the University of Florida's College of Liberal Arts and Sciences, College of Law, African Studies Center and Department of Anthropology. I thank Dean Willard Harrison of CLAS, Deans Jeff Lewis, Richard Matasar, Barry Currier, and George Dawson of the College of Law, Director Michael Chege of the African Studies Center, and past Chairman John Moore of Anthropology for their kind support.

I am grateful, also, to John Mukum Mbaku, the general editor of the Contemporary Perspectives on Developing Countries series, for his encouragement and advice.

Finally, I express my sympathy to the people of Rwanda who have suffered so much through the tragedies of the 1990s. I dedicate this book to them.

1 Comprehending the Rwandan Genocide

Introduction: The Problem

In 1994 Rwanda erupted into one of the most appalling cases of genocide the world had witnessed since World War II. Since genocide is the most aberrant of human behaviors, it cries out for explanation. Why did it occur? In this chapter I offer an analysis and explanation utilizing the human materialism paradigm. A detailed explanation of this paradigm is contained in the book *Human Materialism: A Model of Sociocultural Systems and a Strategy for Analysis* (Magnarella, 1993). Here, I offer only a brief sketch of it.

Human materialism is a systematic paradigm designed to bridge the gap between scientific and humanistic approaches to understanding human behavior, culture, and society. It conceptualizes humans as rational, cost-benefit calculating, scheming, emotional, loving and hating, social creatures who are indoctrinated to some degree in ideological, ritual, and symbolic systems that influence their thought, behavior, and perceptions of their natural and sociocultural environments. Even though human materialism eschews simplistic, reductionistic characteristics of human nature, it still manages to offer a framework or research strategy for investigating human sociocultural systems and generating hypotheses and theories that facilitate understanding, explanation, and prediction.

The human materialist paradigm offers both an abstract model of sociocultural systems and a research strategy. It combines in a unique and fruitful way a number of established theoretical perspectives. One of its major strengths and innovations is its blending of infrastructural causality with humanistic teleology. That is, it places human behavior within its effective environmental context and also focuses significantly on human thought, especially the plans, strategies, and agendas of societal leaders. The paradigm analytically divides sociocultural systems into three major interfacing components–infrastructure, social structure, and superstructure–and suggests, for the purpose of hypothesis formation, a sequence of causal relationships.

Infrastructure is not purely material; it is divided into material, human, and social infrastructural components, and under certain conditions stresses indoctrination and ideology as major causal forces. Social infrastructure includes the effective ownership and control of the forces of production. It consists of the persons in and positions of economic and political power. Such persons are somewhat like orchestra leaders directing available musical resources. By including the persons in positions of power as well as the structural positions they occupy, human materialism assumes that the personality characteristics of powerful individuals must be taken into account. Decisions by elites are not the exclusive result of their structural positions and environmental pressures. Although the model assumes mutual causality within, between, and among the three major components, it hypothesizes that the direction of the more powerful causal forces goes from infrastructure to social structure to superstructure.

Rwanda's Geography

Rwanda, the landlocked 'land of a thousand hills,' consists of only 26,340 square kilometers, making it one of Africa's smallest countries. Its size is comparable to that of Burundi or Belgium or the U.S. state of Maryland. Rwanda's terrain is dominated by mountain ranges (in the west), hills, and highland plateaus. Despite Rwanda's position just south of the equator, its high elevation moderates the climate. Rwanda's neighbors are Uganda (north), Tanzania (east), Burundi (south), and Congo (west).

Throughout the twentieth century, Rwanda's people have placed tremendous pressure on the land. As early as 1983, when Rwanda's population reached 5.5 million, expert observers writing for the Economist Intelligence Unit (hereafter EIU) noted that, 'with the population increasing at an average annual rate of 3.7 per cent, in a country with the highest population density in Africa, the authorities are worried that it will be impossible to increase food sufficiently' (EIU, 1983a, p. 18). At the time, an estimated 95 per cent of the gainfully employed population were engaged in agriculture (EIU, 1983b, p. 28). By 1993, one year before the genocide, the population had climbed to 7.7 million without any substantial improvement in agricultural output. To the contrary, food production had been seriously hampered by periodic drought, overgrazing, soil exhaustion and soil erosion.

Pre-Colonial History

The history of Rwanda prior to German penetration in the late nineteenth century is not well known. One of the first Europeans to explore Rwanda was Count G.A. von Gotzen, a member of an 1894 German scientific-military expedition (Maquet, 1954, p. 164). Historians believe the area's first known inhabitants were a pygmoid people, the hunting-gathering ancestors of the present-day Twa. Around 1,000 AD, Bantu-speaking Hutu horticulturists arrived, probably from the east, and began clearing and settling the hills. Physically, they resembled other Bantu-speakers of central Africa. Their language–Kinyarwanda, a branch of the Niger-Congo subfamily–eventually became the idiom of Rwanda. Hutu became the dominant population, far outnumbering the Twa with whom they bartered agricultural goods for forest products.

Between the eleventh and fifteenth centuries the Tutsi, a pastoral people with long-horned cattle, moved into the region, probably from southern Ethiopia where other pastoralists such as the Oromo resided. Typical of cattle pastoralists, Tutsi men were armed and accustomed to fighting to protect their herds against raiders and to raid themselves for cattle and village goods. Being more aggressive and better organized for military purposes than were the Hutu farmers, the Tutsi eventually conquered central Rwanda and established their rule there. According to Maquet (1961, p. 170), 'Tutsi came into Ruanda as conquerors. ... They wanted to settle in the country and they built a permanent system of economic and political relations with the Hutu whereby they established themselves definitely as masters and exploiters. ... [A] caste society evolved from their will to stabilize the conquest.'

During the reign of Tutsi warrior King (*mwami*) Kigeri Rwabugiri (1860-1895), the Tutsi conquered and firmly established central control over much, but not all, of Rwanda, despite the fact that they represented only about 10 per cent to 14 per cent of a population that was over 80 per cent Hutu. Importantly, a number of Hutu principalities in the north, northwest and southwest remained independent until the late nineteenth and early twentieth centuries (see Prunier, 1997, p. 19; Newbury, 1988). The Tutsi dominated the Hutu and Twa militarily, politically, and economically. According to their common religion, the Tutsi king was a divine and absolute monarch (Maquet, 1961, p. 124). Lemarchand (1970, pp. 33-34) explains:

> The king was the incarnation of the deity (Imana), the embodiment of ancestral virtues, and the source of all prosperity. ... [T]he theme of kingship was inextricably tied up with the theme of Tutsi supremacy. To rebel against the

established order was no less sacrilegious than to rebel against the Mwami himself. According to a popular legend 'the King and the Tutsi [were] the heart of the country. Should the Hutu chase them away, they would lose all they have and the Imana would punish them.'

Theoretically, the king owned all the land and livestock; subjects held usufruct rights (Maquet, 1961, pp. 89-91). Succession to property rights was mainly patrilineal, but the king could and did dispossess subjects of all their property if they displeased or opposed him. King Rwabugiri's rule was harsh and his taxes were heavy. Royal tribute was collected by a group of land chiefs, cattle chiefs, and hill chiefs, who served the king. All cattle chiefs and most land chiefs were Tutsi; Hutu and Twa could serve as hill chiefs (Maquet, 1961, pp. 103-105).

'The dominance of cattle as a form of disposable wealth meant that cattle chiefs–all of them by definition Tutsi–were able to dominate most of Rwanda. To mobilize an army required capital, which came only in the form of livestock, and the Tutsi controlled the cattle' (African Rights, 1995a, p. 4).

In some cases Tutsi royalty ennobled or elevated politically and economically successful Hutu and Twa to the rank of Tutsi. Mbanda (1997, p. 4) writes that 'a Hutu who gained status through wealth or by becoming a chief could become a Tutsi through a ritual of *Kwihutura*--literally, a cleansing of one's Hutuness. ... [I]f a Tutsi lost his cattle and turned to farming for a living and married into a Hutu family, that person could become a Hutu.' No scholar, however, has been able to offer reliable statistics of these kinds of social transformations. Maquet (1961, p. 150) maintains that 'the number of Hutu and Twa assimilated to Tutsi because of the holding of political offices or because of wealth has always been tiny. ... There was no egalitarian ideology. ... Cases of intercaste mobility were extremely rare in Rwanda.'

Some modern historians stress that during the pre-colonial period there were no Tutsi-Hutu conflicts as such. Tutsi and Hutu lived intermingled on the same hills and formed alliances against other groups of allied Hutu and Tutsi. Prunier (1997, p. 39) writes: 'although Rwanda was definitely not a land of peace and bucolic harmony before the arrival of the Europeans, there is no trace in its precolonial history of systematic violence between Tutsi and Hutu as such.' While this may be true, it is important to remember that during the strict reign of Tutsi King Rwabugiri, most of the king's agents were Tutsi and the vast majority of those who suffered were Hutu. Consequently, it is highly probable that many Rwandans believed an effective political cleavage between Tutsi and Hutu did exist.

The Tutsi aristocracy ruled by force, and the army was its main instrument of power. Only Tutsi males were specially trained to be warriors (Maquet 1961, p. 118). Hutu and Twa fought also or acted as auxiliaries who carried supplies, but they did not receive the special Tutsi warrior education. As part of their training, young Tutsi warriors were indoctrinated with an ideology of Tutsi superiority. Their status, military training, and ideology set them apart from non-Tutsi.

Wealthy Tutsi owned large herds of cattle and extensive tracts of land that they had expropriated from the Hutu. By the late nineteenth century many Hutu were experiencing a crippling land crisis and abject poverty (Pottier, 1995, p. 45) As their population grew, increasing numbers of Hutu had insufficient land or none at all. In order to survive they entered into feudal patron-client relations with Tutsi. *Uburetwa* (corvée labor service and offerings of beer in return for access to land) became a principal means of Hutu subjugation. All poor Hutu were bound by *uburetwa*, but Tutsi were exempt (Pottier, 1995, p. 43). For the Hutu, *uburetwa* became the most hated of the feudal contracts (Pottier, 1995, p. 42).

Another feudal contract, the *ubuhake*, could be initiated by a poor man who approached a rich Tutsi and ritually asked for milk or acceptance as the Tutsi's child. If the Tutsi agreed, he granted the poor man, usually a Hutu, protection and usufruct rights over one or more head of cattle. In return, the client or vassal Hutu provided a variety of services to his patron or lord, including cultivating his fields, repairing his huts, and possibly providing him with wives or daughters as concubines (Maquet, 1961. pp. 77, 138). In 1950-51, elderly Tutsi informants told Maquet (1954, p. 177) that by giving one or two cows to a Hutu, 'he becomes our client (*mugaragu*) and then has to do, to a large extent, what we ask of him.' (For a more complete discussion of this contract and its variations, see Prunier, 1997, pp. 13-14).

Given the prevalence of protein-poor diets among the Hutu and the frequent occurrence of drought and famine, they desperately needed access to Tutsi land, milk and the meat from bulls and barren cows. The penalty for stealing cattle was a brutally painful death by impalement. Hence, safe access to cattle was through service contacts with rich and powerful Tutsi, who needed Hutu servants to work their land since they regarded farm labor as degrading.

During the nineteenth century, Tutsi, Hutu, and Twa corresponded roughly to occupational categories. The socioeconomic and political division appeared so rigid to some Western scholars that they referred to it as a caste system. For example, the American anthropologist Helen Codere (1962, p. 48) writes:

Occupational specialization, cultural differences and endogamy justify the use of the term 'caste' for each of these three groups. The Hutu agriculturists also did all manner of menial services for the Tutsi; the Tutsi monopolized all administrative positions and were warriors as well as being pastoralists. The Twa were hunters or potters but in addition they performed a number of special services for the Tutsi: royal dancers and choreographers, musicians, torturers and executioners, pimps, commando raiders, messengers and jesters. Marriages between members of each caste were extremely rare.

A number of modern scholars and early explorers have commented on the physical differences between these three peoples. For example, Codere (1962, p. 48) writes that 'although there has been sufficient intermixture to blur racial lines, the majority of each caste is racially distinct. In stature, for example, the differences are striking: the average stature of the Tutsi is 1 m. 75; the Hutu 1 m. 66; and the Twa 1 m. 55.' Unfortunately, Codere does not reveal the source, time, or sample size of her data. Of the Tutsi, Lemarchand (1970, p. 18) writes that 'physical features suggest obvious ethnic affinities with the Galla tribes of southern Ethiopia.' Duke Frederick of Mecklenburg, who traveled through Central Africa in 1907-08, writes:

> The Watussi [i.e., Tutsi] are a tall, well-made people with an almost ideal physique. Heights of 1.80, 2.00, and even 2.20 meters (from 5 ft. 11 1/2 in. to 7 ft. 2 1/2 in.) are of quite common occurrence, ... their bronze-brown skin reminds one of the inhabitants of the more hilly parts of northern Africa. ... Unmistakable evidences of a foreign strain are betrayed in their high foreheads, the curve of their nostrils, and the fine oval shape of their faces. (1910, pp. 47-48)

His measurements most probably apply only to full grown Tutsi men. By contrast, he described the Twa as a pygmy tribe and the Hutu as a people of medium size 'whose ungainly figures betoken hard toil' (Mecklenburg, 1910, p. 47).

Despite the caste or rigid class structure, there was some genetic mixing among these people as a result of intermarriage and concubineage. Maquet's Hutu informants claimed that marriage between Hutu and Tutsi happened frequently, but his Tutsi informants said they were rare (1961, p. 66). Both groups regarded the idea of marriage with a Twa as insulting. It was not uncommon for rich Tutsi to have Hutu concubines. Maquet (1961, pp. 77-78) maintains that Tutsi fathers gave their unmarried sons the wives and daughters of Hutu clients as concubines. He also writes that Tutsi wives did not accompany their husbands on trips. Instead their husbands took concubines, probably the women of Hutu clients. In addition, Tutsi 'adopted' Hutu children, but many treated them like clients, rather than as their own offspring (Maquet, 1961, pp. 75).

Tutsi notions of superior worth were reflected in the laws they imposed on the parts of Rwanda they controlled. For example, although cattle theft was generally prohibited, a Tutsi could steal cattle from a Hutu with impunity so long as the Hutu had no Tutsi lord or patron to protect him (Maquet, 1954, p. 185). Murder was also generally prohibited, but the penalty for it varied with the classes of the parties. If an ordinary Tutsi murdered a Hutu, the king might authorize the retaliatory killing of one of the murderer's kinsman; if a Hutu murdered a Tutsi, the king would order the killing of two of the murderer's kinsmen (Maquet, 1954, p. 187).

Obviously, Rwanda was not a land of social harmony and equality prior to European colonialization. Based on his review of the historical evidence, Pottier (1995, p. 39) writes that 'ethnic divisions (and "obvious hatred" toward the Tutsi overlords, according to Grogan and Sharp [1900:119]) were well entrenched by 1898, the time the Germans began to colonise Rwanda.'

Pre-Colonial Rwandan Culture

As described above, the social organization of much of pre-colonial Rwanda took the form of a caste or very rigid class structure with limited social mobility. Because Twa, Hutu, and Tutsi were all part of this social system and the culture associated with it, at a high level of abstraction the three peoples shared the same culture. At a lower level of abstraction, however, there were marked inter-caste or inter-class cultural variations. Each of these people possessed their own unique cultural segments of a larger multi-cultural system.

Their shared religion both socially integrated and culturally differentiated them. For example, one common version of the Rwandan origin myth (Maquet, 1954, pp. 173-172) goes as follows: Imana, the maker, created Kazikamuntu–the common ancestor of all humans. Three of Kazikamuntu's children–Gatutsi, Gahutu and Gatwa–became the ancestors of the Tutsi, Hutu, and Twa. Kazikamuntu cursed Gatwa because he had killed one of his brothers. Kazikamuntu originally had chosen Gahutu to be his successor, but because Gahutu fell asleep at an inappropriate time and failed to perform an assigned task, Kazikamuntu turned to Gatutsi, who accomplished the task with sobriety and cleverness. Consequently, Kazikamuntu chose Gatutsi to be the chief of his brothers.

Another myth (Maquet, 1954, pp. 185-186) explains the origins of the Tutsi and Twa differently. It has the Tutsi coming to Rwanda from heaven with a Twa servant. In Rwanda the servant mates with a forest ape, and their offspring become the ancestors of modern Twa–a people many Tutsi regarded as sub-human. Lemarchand (1970, p. 34) writes that from the Rwandan legends of the time 'the Tutsi emerged as Imana's elect, endowed with superior military skill, extraordinary courage, great wealth and commensurate intelligence.'

The customary and preferred diets, or food cultures, of the three peoples also differed. Tutsi preferred dairy products over all else. They also consumed beef and agricultural products, but 'milk [was] the beverage of the high caste. It was considered a complete food, and true Batutsi were said to live on milk alone' (Maquet, 1954, p. 178). Hutu generally had poorer diets. While most consumed mainly agricultural products, those with a *ubuhake* contract had access to limited amounts of milk and meat. Twa ate game meat and traded for agricultural and dairy products.

Leisure-time culture also varied among the three. Maquet (1954, p. 175) writes:

> Enjoyments and the pleasant things in life are very unevenly distributed in Ruanda. ... They [rich Tutsi] do no manual work and have leisure to cultivate eloquence, poetry, refined manners, and the subtle art of being witty when talking and drinking hydromel with friends. Bahutu [i.e., Hutu] ... do not enjoy such gracious living. They have to produce for themselves and for the Batutsi. ... As to the Batwa [i.e., Twa], they are so low in the social hierarchy, and considered so irresponsible that they have had a greater independence of action.

As a result of their exclusive military training and ideological indoctrination, Tutsi men belonged to a fraternity closed to others. Maquet (1954, p. 177) explains:

> [Tutsi] boys at an early age begin their military training which gives them a complete education in the skills, knowledge, and virtues pertaining to their noble condition. This training is given to them as *intore* (chosen ones) at the royal court or at the court of an important chief.

A set of 'caste stereotypes' reinforced the social, economic, and political stratification of Rwandan society. Maquet (1954, p. 185) writes that many Rwandan folktales contained the following characterizations:

Batutsi are intelligent (in the sense of political intrigues), apt to command, refined, courageous, and cruel. Bahutu are hard-working, not very clever, extrovert, irascible, unmannerly, obedient, physically strong. Batwa are gluttonous, loyal to their Batutsi masters, lazy, courageous when hunting, lacking in restraint.

Unflattering as the above is to Hutu and Twa, Maquet (1954, p. 185) goes on to say that 'these characteristics, with differences in stress and shading, are generally recognized by all Banyarwanda [people of Rwanda]. As they reflect the Mututsi point of view, it appears that the superior caste has been able to make other people see themselves in important respects as Batutsi see them.' Maquet (1954, p. 185) claims that the Banyarwanda considered the above qualities to be 'innate, not acquired. A Mututsi is born clever and a Muhutu impulsive. ... Inferiority and superiority are due not to personal qualities but to membership of certain groups.'

German and Belgian Rule

From 1894 until the end of World War I, Rwanda, along with Burundi (similar in population size and 'ethnic' composition to Rwanda) and present-day Tanzania was part of German East Africa. Belgium claimed it thereafter, and in 1924 Belgium became the administering authority under the League of Nations mandate system. Belgium ruled Rwanda and Burundi (then called the Territory of Ruanda-Urundi) as a single administrative trusteeship until 1962. By then, the two countries had evolved different political systems. Hutu political leaders declared Rwanda a republic in January 1961 and forced the Tutsi monarch, Kigeri, into exile. Burundi, by contrast, remained a constitutional monarchy until 1966.

During their colonial tenure, the Germans chose to rule Rwanda indirectly through the existing Tutsi monarch (*mwami*) and his chiefs. This had the effect of continuing the 'pre-colonial transformation towards more centralisation, annexation of the Hutu principalities and increase in Tutsi chiefly power' (Prunier, 1997, p. 25). 'Mutually advantageous relations were the result: the Germans used [Tutsi king] Musinga to establish their authority in the northwest of the colony; Musinga used the Germans to strengthen his own position in Ruanda' (Louis, 1963, p. 122). The principal means by which the Germans maintained authority was the often brutal punitive expedition. Louis (1963, p. 203) explains:

> When a chief refused to submit to German rule, or, especially in Ruanda, to the authority of the mwami, a German officer would set out to destroy systematically the villages and agriculture of the 'rebel' and would appropriate his cattle. In the most serious cases,...the main offenders were hanged.

The early Europeans were generally impressed with the ruling Tutsi. Reasoning from the premises of Social Darwinism, an evolutionary theory prevalent in Europe at the time, many Europeans believed that Tutsi political and economic success evinced their superior fitness in the struggle for survival. Because the Tutsi ruled over the Hutu and Twa, Europeans concluded that they were indeed, like the colonialists themselves, a people superior to common Africans. In fact, some Europeans concluded, the Tutsi were not really sub-Saharan Africans at all, but rather a Hamitic people, probably descendants of the ancient Egyptians. Hence, the colonialists developed the 'Hamitic myth' which held that the Tutsi and everything humanly superior in Central Africa came from ancient Egypt or Abyssinia. The Europeans made it known to the people of Ruanda-Urundi that they regarded Hutu and Twa as inferior to Tutsi. Prunier (1997, p. 9) writes that sixty years of such prejudicial fabrications 'ended by inflating the Tutsi cultural ego inordinately and crushing Hutu feelings until they coalesced into an aggressively resentful inferiority complex.'

The Belgians initially favored the Tutsi over the Hutu even more than the Germans had. Belgian administrators replaced Hutu chiefs with Tutsi. The replacement policy was so extensive that by 1959, 43 out of 45 chiefs and 549 of 559 sub-chiefs were Tutsi (Destexhe, 1995, p. 40). In addition, '83 per cent of posts in such areas as the judiciary, agriculture and veterinary services' were held by Tutsi (Kamukama, 1997, p. 21).

Initially Christian missionaries spread their religion to the more receptive Hutu, since the Tutsi king and aristocracy rejected it. Christian theology had the effect of discrediting the indigenous belief in the Tutsi king's divine nature; it also prohibited polygyny, a practice common among rich Tutsi and Hutu. By contrast, poor and marginal Hutu regarded the European churches as their new, protective patrons. By 1930, however, some of the Tutsi realized that to remain part of the elite in a Rwanda dominated by Christian Belgians, they, too, had to convert. The process of Tutsi conversion accelerated after 1931 when the Belgians deposed King Yuhi Musinga and replaced him with his son. The old king had been an unchanageable native. By contrast, his son dressed in Western clothes, drove a car and converted to Christianity (Prunier 1997, p. 31). Henceforth, the Christian schools, both Catholic and Protestant, had much larger Tutsi than Hutu enrollments.

In order to profit from their colonial investment, the Belgians instituted a number of agricultural and infrastructural projects (e.g., coffee cultivation, terracing, road building and maintenance, construction of railway lines, etc.) that required a huge amount of cheap or free native labor. Hence, they redesigned the traditional corvée system so that every man had to contribute time and energy to government-designated projects. Those who failed to meet government expectations were often brutally beaten by enforcers appointed by local Tutsi chiefs. According to Lemarchand (1970, pp. 123-124), of 250 Rwandans, mostly Hutu, interviewed by a member of a UN Visiting Mission in 1948, 247 said they had been whipped and 245 claimed to have been sent to prison for failure to perform government-ordered work.

The people grew to hate the forced labor requirement, the brutal punishments and the government functionaries (usually Tutsi) who applied them. 'Nothing so vividly defined the divide [between Tutsi and Hutu] as the Belgian regime of forced labor, which required armies of Hutus to toil en masse as plantation chattel, on road construction, and in forestry crews, and placed Tutsis over them as taskmasters' (Gourevitch, 1998a, p. 57). The Tutsi compradors directed the corvée laborers with whips. If the Tutsi supervisors did not get the job done, their white colonial masters whipped and replaced them. Corvée work demands were so great that they could consume 50 per cent to 60 per cent of a native's time (Prunier, 1997, p. 35). This huge amount of labor, having been forcibly diverted from the production of food, most probably contributed to the famine of 1940-1945. Due to the brutal Belgian regime, land shortages, and famine, 'hundreds of thousands of Hutus and impoverished rural Tutsis fled north to Uganda and west to the Congo to seek their fortunes as itinerant agricultural laborers' (Gourevitch, 1998a, p. 57).

During 1933-34 the Belgians conducted a census and introduced an identity card system that indicated the Tutsi, Hutu, or Twa 'ethnicity' (*ubwoko* in Kinyarwanda and *ethnie* in French) of each person. However, the Belgians 'decided to classify any individual [i.e., farmer] with fewer than ten cows as a Hutu' (Vassal-Adams, 1994. p. 8). According to African Rights (1995a, p. 9), the Belgians used 'ownership of cows as the key criterion for determining which group an individual belonged to. Those with ten or more cows were Tutsi–along with all their descendants in the male line–and those with less were Hutu. Those "recognized as Twa" at the time of the census were given the status of Twa.' This basis for classification contributed to the physical mix found in each of the various 'ethnic' categories which, taken together, the census determined to be 85 per cent Hutu, 14 per cent Tutsi, and one per cent Twa.

The identity card 'ethnicity' of future generations was determined patrilineally; all persons were designated as having the 'ethnicity' of their fathers, regardless of the 'ethnicity' of their mothers. This practice, which was carried on until its abolition by the 1994 post-genocide government, had the unfortunate consequence of firmly attaching a sub-national identity to all Rwandans and thereby rigidly dividing them into categories, which, for many people, carried a negative history of dominance-subordination, superiority-inferiority, and exploitation-suffering. In their 'Hutu Manifesto' of 1957 (discussed below), Hutu leaders referred to the identity card categories as 'races' (Prunier, 1997, pp. 45-46), thereby evincing how inflexible these labels had become in their minds.

The Transformation to Independence

Belgium altered its policy of discrimination in the late 1950s to favor the Hutu. A variety of causes contributed to this change. As Gourevitch (1998a, p. 58) points out, Belgium itself had been divided along ethnic lines, with the Francophone Walloon minority historically dominating the Flemish majority. After World War II newly arrived Flemish missionaries to Rwanda identified with the suppressed Hutu and supported their political aspirations. In accordance with UN General Assembly Resolution 1413(XIV) of 1959, Belgium set 1962 as the target date for the independence of Ruanda-Urundi. Foreseeing the inevitable dominance of the Hutu majority, Belgian colonial administrators sided with them, claiming to promote a democratic revolution.

In 1957, a group of nine Hutu intellectuals had published the so-called 'Hutu Manifesto,' which complained of the political, economic, and educational monopoly of the Tutsi 'race' and characterized the Tutsi as foreign invaders. The Manifesto called for promoting Hutu in all fields and argued for the maintenance of 'ethnic' identity cards so as to monitor the race monopoly (Lemarchand, 1970, p. 149). Tutsi royalty rejected the Manifesto and blamed colonial administrators for any interethnic problems. The monarchists also advocated 'the eviction of the trust authorities at the earliest possible date, so as to reassert their control over the destinies of the country' (Lemarchand, 1970. p. 153).

Political activists formed a series of pro-Tutsi, pro-Hutu, and integrationist parties. 'But the political struggle in Rwanda was never really a quest for equality; the issue was only who would dominate the ethnically bipolar state' (Gourevitch, 1998a, p. 58). In November 1959, the pro-Hutu PARMEHUTU party led a revolt that resulted in bloody ethnic clashes and the toppling of King Kigri V. Beginning in 1960, the colonial administrators began replacing Tutsi chiefs with Hutu, who immediately led persecution campaigns against the Tutsi living on the hills the Hutu now controlled. By 1963, these and other Hutu attacks had resulted in thousands of Tutsi deaths and the flight of about 130,000 Tutsi to neighboring countries, with 50,000 going to Burundi (Prunier, 1997, pp. 51, 55). The land and cattle that the fleeing Tutsi left behind were quickly claimed by land-hungry Hutu.

Belgian authorities organized communal elections in mid-1960. The PARMEHUTU and other pro-Hutu parties won the vast majority of posts. Of 229 mayoral (*bourgmestre*) positions, only 19 were Tutsi, and 160 were PARMEHUTU (Prunier, 1997. p. 52). As a result of the national election held under UN supervision in 1961, Gregoire Kayibanda (an author of the 'Hutu Manifesto') became Rwanda's president-designate. Kayibanda, the son of Hutu farmers, had studied for the priesthood at a Catholic seminary and had been employed as a secretary by a Belgian bishop. By 1960, he had become a leader of the PARMEHUTU. Being married to a Tutsi woman did not deter him from presiding over vicious attacks on Tutsi (Nyankanzi, 1998, p. 134).

As a result of a referendum, Rwanda was declared independent on 1 July 1962. President Kayibanda soon established a style of rule that resembled that of the traditional Tutsi kings. He became remote, secretive, and authoritarian. His demand for 'unquestioning obedience was to play a tragic and absolutely central role in the unfolding of the 1994 genocide' (Prunier, 1997, p. 57).

Supported by the Tutsi-dominated government in Burundi, Rwandan Tutsi refugees there began launching unsuccessful attacks into Rwanda. These invasions were usually followed by brutal Hutu reprisals against local Tutsi. The Hutu government used a failed 1963 invasion as the pretext 'to launch a massive wave of repression in which an estimated 10,000 Tutsi were slaughtered between December 1963 and January 1964. All surviving Tutsi politicians still living in Rwanda were executed' (Prunier, 1997, p. 56). Lemarchand (1970, p. 44) writes the following about this period:

> The recent history of Rwanda is punctuated with countless examples of bloodshed and violence; but there are no precedents for the appalling brutality employed after independence by some Hutu officials. In late 1963 and early 1964 thousands of innocent Tutsi were wantonly murdered in what has been described as a genocide. ... [T]he scale and methods by which it was perpetrated suggest that it can only be regarded as an extreme example of pathological behavior, as the blind reaction of a people traumatised by a deep and lasting sense of inferiority.

The Rwandan situation was exacerbated by events in neighboring Burundi. In the spring of 1972 some Burundian Hutu rebelled against the Tutsi military regime. The regime put down the rebellion and then embarked on a campaign to eliminate educated Burundian Hutu. A genocide frenzy ensued; about 100,000 Hutu were killed and another 200,000 fled for their lives, many into Rwanda. President Kayibanda capitalized on the situation by eliminating several hundred Rwandan Tutsi in the name of public safety and sending another 100,000 fleeing out of the country as refugees. Consequently, more Tutsi land and cattle were taken over by rural Hutu.

Kayibanda's government had earlier installed an ethnic quota system whereby the proportion of Tutsi in schools, civil service, and other employment sectors was officially limited to nine per cent, their under-estimated proportion of the general population. On occasion, but especially in 1972-73, Hutu 'vigilante committees ... scrutinised the schools, the University, the civil service and even private businesses to make sure that the ethnic quota policy was being respected. Those eager to carry out this "purification"...were educated people who could expect to benefit from kicking the Tutsi out of their jobs' (Prunier, 1997, p. 60).

The Second Republic

In July 1973, Major Juvénal Habyarimana, a northern Hutu, overthrew Kayibanda, a southerner, and declared himself president of the Second Republic. Over the next few years, his security forces would eliminate former president Kayibanda and many of his high ranking supporters as part of a plan to eradicate serious Hutu opposition. Habyarimana's kin and regional supporters filled high level positions in the government and security forces. Close relatives of the president and his wife dominated the army, gendarmerie and, especially, the Presidential Guard.

Habyarimana's Rwanda became a single-party dictatorship. His party, the *Mouvement Révolutionnaire National pour le Développement* (MRND), was enshrined in the constitution. He relegated the Tutsi to the private sector. 'Throughout the Habyarimana years there would not be a single Tutsi *bourgmestre* or *préfet*; there was only one Tutsi officer in the whole army, there were two Tutsi members of parliament out of seventy and there was only one Tutsi minister out of a cabinet of between twenty-five and thirty members' (Prunier, 1997, p. 75). Regulations prohibited army members from marrying

Tutsi. Habyarimana also maintained the 'ethnic' identity card and 'ethnic' quota systems of the previous regime.

Up until 1990, when the Tutsi-dominated Rwandese Popular Front (RPF) army invaded from Uganda, Rwanda's main internal political issue was the north/south divide. 'Habyarimana had consistently favoured his home region in the north-west. The north received a disproportionate share of resources, and northerners enjoyed better educational opportunities and were over-represented in government and state companies. The leading advocates of change within Rwanda were Hutu from the south, who felt they were entitled to a greater share of the country's resources' (Vassal-Adams, 1994. p. 23).

The principal foreign issue concerned refugees. By the mid-1980s, the number of Rwandan refugees in neighboring countries has surpassed one-half million. Thousands more were living in Europe and North America. Habyarimana adamantly refused to allow their return, insisting that Rwanda was already too crowded and had too little land, jobs, and food for them (Vassal-Adams, 1994, p. 10). However, the surrounding countries were also poor and had insufficient resources to accommodate both their own citizens and large refugee populations (Mbanda, 1997, p. 74).

Many Rwandan Tutsi refugees in Uganda joined forces with the Ugandan revolutionary Yoweri Museveni, helping him to overthrow the government of Milton Obote in 1986. In the process they received military training, and a few became high-ranking officers in the Ugandan military. Together with some Rwandese Hutu refugees, they formed the RPF and committed themselves to return to Rwanda. In 1990-92 RPF troops conducted a number of assaults into Rwanda from Uganda in unsuccessful attempts to seize power. The fighting caused the displacement of hundreds of thousands of people. Habyarimana retaliated by heightening internal repression against Tutsi. His security forces indiscriminately interned and persecuted Tutsi solely because of their ethnic identity, claiming they were actual or potential accomplices of the RPF (Jefremovas, 1995, pp. 28-29; Newbury, 1995, pp. 12-14). From 1990 to 1992 Hutu ultra-nationalists killed an estimated 2000 Tutsi; they also targeted human rights advocates, regardless of their ethnicities (Newbury, 1995, p. 15).

The slaughter of Tutsi was not solely the result of RPF threats from the north. Radical indoctrination also played a role. In April 1990, six months before the RPF's October invasion, President Habyarimana attended a Franco-African summit in France. French President François Mitterrand, one of Habyarimana's supporters, advised the Rwandan president to permit multi-party politics. Habyarimana quickly did so, thereby allowing a platform for political groups, such as the *Coalition pour la Défense de la République* (CDR), that were even more radically pro-Hutu and 'racist' than his own MRND. Hasan Ngeze, a CDR member and Hutu supremacist, became a major preacher of anti-Tutsi hatred. In the sixth issue (December 1990) of his newspaper, *Kangura*, he vilified the Tutsi in his infamous 'Ten Commandments of the Hutu.' The most inflammatory and discriminatory of these were the following:

1) Every Hutu must know that a Tutsi woman, wherever she may be, is working in the pay of her Tutsi ethnicity. Therefore, a traitor is any Hutu who marries a Tutsi woman, makes a Tutsi his concubine, or makes a Tutsi his secretary or protégé.
4) Every Hutu must know that every Tutsi is dishonest in business. He aims only at the supremacy of his ethnicity. Therefore, a traitor is any Hutu: Who makes an alliance with the Tutsi in his business; Who invests his money or the money of the state in the enterprise of a Tutsi; Who extends business favors to the Tutsi (the granting of importation licenses, bank loans, construction packages, public markets).
5) Strategic posts such as political, administrative, economic, military, and security posts must be given to the Hutu only.
7) The Armed Forces of Rwanda must be exclusively Hutu. No member of the military should marry a Tutsi.
8) The Hutu must stop feeling pity for the Tutsi.
9) The Hutu, wherever they may be, must be united, show solidarity, and be preoccupied with the fate of their Hutu brethren. The Hutu must be firm and vigilant in their enmity against their common Tutsi enemy.
10) The 1959 Social Revolution, the 1961 Referendum, and the Hutu ideology must be taught to every Hutu at all levels. Every Hutu must widely propagate the current ideology. (Chrétien, 1995, pp. 39-40)

The 'Ten Commandments' circulated widely and became a major anti-Tutsi indoctrination text. 'Community leaders across Rwanda regarded them as tantamount to law, and read them aloud at public meetings' (Gourevitch, 1998a, p. 88). The eighth commandment–'The Hutu must stop feeling pity for the Tutsi'–would be invoked mercilessly during the 1994 genocide.

The Arusha Accords

Rwanda's 1990-92 war with the RPF occurred while the country was experiencing a financial and economic crisis. At the urging of the Organization of African Unity and some West European governments, Habyarimana agreed to a series of meetings with RPF representatives in Arusha, Tanzania, to negotiate peace and a new governmental plan for Rwanda. Despite strong opposition from the growing right-wing and ultra-racist Hutu Power movement in Rwanda, Habyarimana's government signed a series of agreements with the RPF. These included accords for a cease-fire, a power-sharing government, return of refugees to Rwanda, and integration of the armed forces. In addition to allowing hundreds of thousands of Tutsi to return to Rwanda, the RPF was to constitute 40 per cent of the integrated military forces and 50 per cent of its officer corps. It would also be allotted five ministries (including the important Interior Ministry) in a broad-based government (Prunier, 1997, pp. 192-193). Habyarimana's own MRND would be allocated only five ministries and eleven MPs in the new 70-member National Assembly. The presidency would become largely ceremonial. The final accord was signed on 3 August 1993.

Gourevitch correctly notes that for Habyarimana the Arusha Accords amounted to a suicide note. After enjoying exclusive power for twenty years, Hutu Power leaders could never accept these changes. 'They cried treason, and charged that the President himself had become an "accomplice"' (Gourevitch, 1998a, pp. 99). If the Accords were implemented, many Hutu elitists in government and in the military would lose their privileged positions. A significant number of northern Hutu related to or allied with the powerful lineage of Habyarimana's wife were among those who would be adversely affected. Within days of the signing, *Radio Milles Collines*, a new, private station devoted to genocidal propaganda, began broadcasting anti-Accord and anti-Tutsi diatribes from Kigali.

Bill Berkeley (1998), a veteran correspondent covering Africa, wrote the following about this period in Rwanda:

> Habyarimana ran lucrative rackets in everything from development aid to marijuana smuggling. He and his in-laws operated the country's black market foreign exchange bureau in tandem with the Central Bank. Habyarimana was implicated in the poaching of mountain gorillas, selling the skulls and feet of baby primates. His brother-in-law was the main suspect in the murder of American anthropologist Diane Fossey. This was the mafia-like culture in which the genocide was hatched.

Events in Burundi

Events to the south, in neighboring Burundi, contributed to the call in Rwanda for Hutu power and Tutsi elimination. After nearly thirty years of Tutsi dictatorship in Burundi, the people participated in the country's first free election in July 1993 and chose Hutu Melchior Ndadaye as their president. Ndadaye headed FRODEBU (*Front pour la democracy au Burundi*), a political organization whose roots go back to the 1972 Burundian refugees in Rwanda (Lemarchand, 1996, p. 143). 'Motivated by a deep hatred for the Tutsi-dominated army [in Burundi] and the 1972 massacre [of Burundian Hutu], the Hutu overwhelmingly voted for FRODEBU' in the 1993 election (Nyankanzi, 1998, p. 43).

Many Burundi Tutsi, however, regarded the election as a Hutu victory, rather than as a majority decision. They felt threatened by the new president's stated policy of proportional 'ethnic' representation in schools, the army, and government employment, and his intention to retire senior (i.e., Tutsi) military officers. On 21 October 1993, a contingent of the Tutsi-dominated army attacked the presidential palace, killing the president, his family, and several of his political associates. Some members of his cabinet sought refuge in the Rwandan Embassy.

Leaders of FRODEBU immediately urged Hutu citizens to kill any Tutsi they could get their hands on. Four ministers in Ndadaye's cabinet used Radio-Kigali in Rwanda for their genocide message (Lemarchand, 1996, p. xv). 'Hutu hoodlums took revenge on innocent Tutsi throughout the countryside. Armed with machetes, spears, knives, and clubs, they roamed from village to village and house to house, hacking every Tutsi in sight. Churches and schools were transformed into killing fields' (Nyankanzi, 1998, p. 46). The Tutsi-dominated Burundi army responded by killing Hutu, in its efforts 'to restore peace.' Altogether, about 50,000 people were murdered, and approximately 375,000 Burundians, mostly Hutu, fled into Rwanda for safety.

Members of Rwanda's Hutu Power movement and President Habyarimana, who had been close to Burundian President Ndadaye, became alarmed by these events. Consequently, they refused to implement the Arusha Accords and integrate refugee Tutsi back into the country. 'The 1993 crisis in Burundi, like previous crises such as the genocide [of Burundian Hutu] of 1972, had a catastrophic impact on Hutu-Tutsi relations in Rwanda. ... The message conveyed by the assassination [of Ndadaye] was "never trust the Tutsi"' (Igwara, 1995, p. 11).

'Genocide [of Tutsi] came to be seen increasingly by MNRD politicians as the only rational option, and compromise, along the lines of Arusha, as synonymous with political suicide' (Lemarchand, 1995, p. 10). The MNRD and CDR had begun training and indoctrinating anti-Tutsi youth militias, known respectively as the *Interahamwe* ('Those who attack together') and *Impuzamugambi* ('Those with a single purpose'). They would soon become vicious death squads. Hutu extremists drew up death lists containing the names of prominent Tutsi and Hutu political opponents. Attacks on Tutsi and Hutu who supported the Arusha Accords became commonplace.

Assassination and Genocide

Fearing that the reigning instability in Rwanda would threaten the region, the heads of the surrounding states pressured Habyarimana to honor the Arusha Accords. During a regional meeting of heads of state in Dar-es-Salaam, Tanzania, President Yoweri Museveni of Uganda and President Ali Hassan Mwinyi of Tanzania appeared to have won a commitment from Habyarimana that he would indeed begin implementing the accords. On 6 April 1994, however, as Habyarimana's presidential plane neared the Kigali Airport on his return from Dar-es-Salam, it was struck by a missile and plunged to earth, killing the president and all aboard.

Although the identity of his assassins is not known, many foreign observers believe Habyarimana was killed by Hutu extremists in his own military, the *Forces Armées Rwandaises* (FAR), a Hutu institution that may have had the most to lose from the Arusha agreements.[1] Only a month before, the Hutu Power publication, *Kangura*, had run the banner headline 'Habyarimana will die in March.' The same issue carried a 'cartoon depicting the President as a Tutsi-loving RPF accomplice' (Gourevitch, 1998a, pp. 108).

'Within the hour following the crash, and prior to its official announcement over the radio, Interahamwe militiamen had begun to set up road-blocks in Kigali. During 6 and 7 April, the young men checked the identity cards of passers-by, searching for Tutsi, members of opposition parties, and human rights activists. Anyone belonging to these groups was set upon with machetes and iron bars. Their bleeding bodies lined the roads of the city' (Vassal-Adams, 1994, p. 32). The Presidential Guard began killing Tutsi civilians in Ramera, a section of Kigali near the airport. *Radio Milles Collines* blamed the RPF and a contingent of UN soldiers for Habyarimana's death and urged revenge against the Tutsi. Extremists in the president's entourage had made up lists of Hutu political opponents, mostly democrats, for the first wave of murders.

> The assassins' first priority was to eliminate Hutu opposition leaders,... After that, the wholesale extermination of Tutsis got underway, ... With the encouragement of [radio] messages and leaders at every level of society, the slaughter of Tutsis and the assassination of Hutu oppositionists spread from region to region. Following the militias' example, Hutus young and old rose to

the task. Neighbors hacked neighbors to death in their homes, and colleagues hacked colleagues to death in their workplaces. Doctors killed their patients, and schoolteachers killed their pupils. Within days, the Tutsi populations of many villages were all but eliminated, ... Radio announcers reminded listeners not to take pity on women and children. (Gourevitch, 1998a, pp. 114-15)

The approximately 1,500-man Presidential Guard (GP) was responsible for the assassination of hundreds of political opponents. 'The French government played a key role in organizing, training and arming the GP. From 1990 until late 1993, French military advisors were present in Rwanda, attached to the GP. The GP itself played a key role in organizing, training and arming the interahamwe militias' (African Rights, 1995a, p. 49). In turn, the Interahamwe recruited and trained Hutu refugees from Burundi, who earned reputations for their extreme brutality (African Rights, 1995a, pp. 63-64).

One of the most depressing accounts of the slaughter is the African Rights publication sub-titled *When Women Become Killers*. It describes the general participation in the genocide:

> The killings would never have claimed so many lives if the killers had not adopted a strategy to involve as much of the population as possible–men, women and even children as young as eight. The hundred days' genocide was no spontaneous outburst. It followed instructions from the highest levels of the political, military and administrative hierarchies. At an intermediate level, huge numbers of [people from all occupations] were involved, both directly and indirectly.
>
> Some women, including young girls in their teens, were participants in the carnage, hacking other women and children, and sometimes even men, to death. Some of these women joined willingly. Others were forced in the same manner that men were forced, ... They participated in massacres and in the murder of their neighbours as well as strangers. They joined the crowds that surrounded churches, hospitals and other places of refuge, wielding machetes, nail-studded clubs and spears...Above all, women and girls stripped the dead–and the barely living–stealing their jewelry, money and clothes. (African Rights, 1995b, pp. 1-2)

The organizers of the massacres wanted to create a new Rwanda, a community of murderers, who shared a collective sense of accomplishment or guilt. The new Rwandans would undergo an initiation rite by killing their former neighbors. In the process, they would take on a new identity and shared responsibility for the killings. What would have been crimes under ordinary circumstances, became expected and common behavior.

The extremists exhorted the Interahamwe and ordinary Hutu to kill Tutsi and 'eat their cows.' The later phrase had both symbolic and practical significance. Symbolic, because historically Tutsi supremacy had been built on cattle ownership. 'Eating their cows' meant devouring the basis of Tutsi past dominance. Practical, because it also meant looting Tutsi homes, farms, offices, business, churches, and so on. 'Theft was one of the principal weapons used to bribe people into betraying and killing their neighbors' (African Rights, 1995a, pp. 1002-1003). Some Hutu leaders urged their followers 'to send the Tutsi back to their country of origin, Ethiopia, by the quickest route, via the Akanyaru river' (Lemarchand, 1995, p. 62). Consequently some northerly flowing rivers were filled with the dead. People in Uganda recovered about 40,000 bodies from Lake Victoria and buried them (Prunier, 1997, p. 255).

The murderers were not content with simply killing Tutsi and Hutu rivals, they expended a great deal of time and effort torturing and mutilating their victims. The murderers enjoyed watching the suffering and agony. They often chopped off their victim's long fingers, small noses, and shapely breasts–the physical symbols of Tutsiness. They hacked off Tutsi penises as if to disempower their historic rulers. Some victims were burnt alive. Rape was used extensively, even against wounded women. The psychological need to eliminate the Tutsi was so great, that Hutu extremists hunted down and killed the pregnant Hutu wives of Tutsi men, so that their 'Tutsi' fetuses would not survive (*Prosecutor v. Akayesu*, 1998). The Rwandan interim government portrayed the situation to the media as 'a spontaneous outbreak of tribal violence' (African Rights, 1995a, p. 250).

RPF troops from the north began fighting their way south in early April in an attempt to stop the slaughter. 'But the RPF's advance simply could not match the pace at which the militiamen and soldiers were massacring civilians' (Vassal-Adams, 1994, p. 37). The RPF took Kigalai on July 4th and Butare, the second-largest city, on July 5th. By July 18, the RPF had reached the Zairian border, having captured the town of Gisenyi the previous day. Having defeated the Hutu FAR and militias that opposed them, the RPF unilaterally declared a cease-fire.

Within a period of only three months approximately 800,000 Tutsi and between 10,000 to 30,000 Hutu or 11 per cent of the total population had been killed (Prunier 1997:265). This Rwandan tragedy may have set an historic record for the largest number of people killed in such a short time. About two million people were uprooted within Rwanda, while the same number of Hutu fled from Rwanda into Tanzania, Burundi, and Zaire. Many were driven out by remnants of FAR and Hutu militias that planned to rearm and organize the refugees into a fighting force that they hoped would re-enter Rwanda and finish the job.

The RPF and moderate Hutu political parties formed a new government on 18 July 1994, but the country was in chaos. The government pledged to implement the Arusha peace agreement on power sharing previously reached by Habyarimana's regime and the RPF on 3 August 1993. On 10 August 1995, the UN Security Council called upon the new Rwandan government to ensure that there would be no reprisals against Hutu wishing to return to their homes and resume their work, reminded the government of its responsibility for a national reconciliation, and emphasized that the Arusha Peace Accords constituted an appropriate framework for reconciliation (UN Doc. S/PRST/1994/42).

The new Rwandan government was a coalition of twenty-two ministers drawn from the RPF (with nine ministers) and four other political parties. Both Tutsi and Hutu were among the top government officials. Pasteur Bizimungu, a Hutu, was named president, while Paul Kagame, a Tutsi, was appointed vice-president and minister of defense. Faustin Twagiramungu, a Hutu, was prime minister until late August 1995, when he was replaced by Pierre Claver Rwigema, also a Hutu. The government publicly committed itself to building a multiparty democracy and to discontinuing the ethnic classification system utilized by the previous regime (Bonner, 1994).

Causes of Genocide

When analyzing major events in complex political societies, such as states, the human materialist paradigm or research strategy recommends an initial focus on the material, demographic, and leadership sub-components of infrastructure as potential causal variables. In the case of Rwanda, the interaction of these infrastructural components led to the genocide. Rwanda was faced with a critical food-people-land imbalance.

In the years leading up to the genocide there had been a marked decline of kilocalories per person per day and overall farm production (André and Platteau, 1998, p. 3). Famines occurred in the late 1980s and early 1990s in several parts of the country (*ibid.*). Emergency sources of food in neighboring countries also were limited. Seavoy (1989, pp. 85-86), writing generally about famine in East Africa, notes that 'hunger is endemic among all peasant societies in East Africa. ... Malnutrition often affects one-third of a village's population.'

'In some areas population densities exceeded 400 people per square kilometer–over 1000 per square mile. In many parts of the country, the average family had scarcely half a hectare of land, while increasing amounts of land were being taken over by the wealthy. Youths faced a situation where many (perhaps most) had no land, no jobs, little education, and no hope for a future' (Newbury, 1995, pp. 14-15). Without a house and a source of livelihood, they could not marry.

The previous historical sections discuss the political foundations of Hutu-Tutsi distinctions and antagonisms. Importantly, while these people may have lived together relatively peacefully prior to the mid-nineteenth century, that was a time when their total population was comparatively low (probably less than two million, versus over seven million in 1993) and land supply for both farming and cattle grazing was ample. With rapid population growth in the twentieth century, the situation changed.[2]

Because of their historically different modes of ecological adaptation–Hutu horticulture and Tutsi cattle pastoralism–within the context of a society over 90 per cent agrarian, a rapidly growing rural population, no significant employment alternatives, and diminishing food production and consumption per capita, the Hutu and Tutsi became natural competitors. Those Tutsi still engaged in cattle pastoralism wanted open ranges to graze their herds. In direct opposition, landless Hutu wanted those very lands, marginal as they may have been for agriculture, to build homesteads on and to farm.

By flight or death of more than half of Rwanda's Tutsi population from the early 1960s to 1973, vast tracts of land in the eastern region were freed up for Hutu settlement and cultivation (André and Platteau, 1998, p. 4). The political elites exploited these developments, which appeared to prove that Hutu farmers could have sufficient land if the Tutsi were eliminated. By the mid-1980s population increases had again outstripped the amount of cultivable land. Farmers' attempts to increase food production by double- and triple-cropping their dwindling plots resulted in soil exhaustion. While foreign experts looked for means of increasing the country's food production potential, they usually had to admit that they are impressed by the relative sophistication of the traditional intensive methods of farming (EIU, 1983a, p. 18). 'Research efforts to-date have not succeeded in developing more than a few varieties of traditional food crops that are more productive and resistant than local varieties' (André and Platteau, 1998, p. 4). Foreign technical experts could do little to help farmers; the problem was the increasing imbalance of the land:people ratio.

There were few employment alternatives to farming. The country's major employer was the government. In the late 1980s, the central government was employing 7,000 people and the local governments 43,000 (Vassal-Adams, 1994, p. 12). By law, only nine per cent of these employees could be Tutsi. Eliminating the Tutsi would open up 4,500 more government jobs for Hutu.

Because the country had no social security program, the thousands of unemployed young people who entered the job market each year lived on the very margins of survival (*Ibid.*). Many became easy subjects for recruitment and manipulation. 'In Kigali the *Interahamwe* and the *Impuzamugambi* tended to recruit mostly among the poor. As soon as they went into action, they drew around them a cloud of even poorer people, a *lumpenproletariat* of street boys, rag-pickers, car-washers and homeless unemployed. For these people the genocide was the best thing that could ever happen to them. ... They could steal, they could kill with minimum justification, they could rape and they could get drunk for free' (Prunier, 1997, p. 232).

'Before the [1994] war a statistically significant relationship was found between regional variations in the incidence of juvenile delinquency on the one hand, and regional variations in per capita availability of calories on the other. As a matter of fact, together with population density, the latter variable explained as much as 58 per cent of the regional variations in offences committed by persons between 21 and 15 years old' (André and Platteau, 1998, p. 37, citing Maton, 1994, pp. 27-28).

'It is not frivolous to conclude that economic desperation, blighting individuals' presents and their perceived futures, was a major contributor to the willingness of many thousands of poor farmers and urban dwellers (a) to fear the possibility of a Tutsi land- and jobs-grab under a victorious RPF regime, (b) to be tempted by more specific hopes for land and jobs, or, more crudely still, to participate in order to grab a share of the victims' property' (Austin, 1996, p. 10, as quoted in André and Platteau, 1998, pp. 38-39).

As stated above, Habyarimana had adamantly refused to allow Tutsi refugees back into the country, insisting that Rwanda was too small and too crowded to accommodate them. What did ordinary people think about the country's demographics? According to André and Platteau (1998, p. 40), 'It is not rare, even today, to hear Rwandans argue that a war is necessary to wipe out an excess of population and to bring numbers into line with the available land resources.'

Despite the country's significant infrastructural problems, the economists André and Platteau correctly conclude that the 'extreme scarcity of land resources and lack of non-agricultural employment opportunities did not (directly) cause the civil war that was triggered off by macro-political forces cynically playing upon ethnic divisions in order to maintain themselves in power. Yet, there can be no doubt that the strained situation engendered by economic scarcities goes a long way towards explaining why violence spread so quickly and so devastatingly throughout the countryside' (André and Platteau, 1998, p. 38).

The human materialist research strategy recommends taking into account also the strategies of Hutu leaders to determine to what extent they contributed to the genocide. In this poor country, regional Hutu elites vied with each other to acquire the economic resources, especially tax revenue and foreign aid, that the reins of political power controlled. Their common plan involved marginalizing the educated Tutsi to eliminate any domestic competition from them and demonizing all Tutsi so as to dupe poor Hutu, the vast majority of the population, into believing that the elites protected them and represented their interests. With the Tutsi sidelined, Hutu regional elites competed with each other.

Rwanda's poor economy rests on peasant subsistence agriculture. The governing elite could extract only limited surplus value directly from the peasant masses. In addition to taxes, the governing elite had two other potential sources of enrichment: skimming export revenues and foreign aid. During the late 1980s and early 1990s the three sources of export earnings–coffee, tea, and tin–all declined. According to a UN source, the tin mining company set up by Rwanda's government in 1990 was losing about $5 million a year (EIU 1993a, p. 25). The mine itself had been closed in the mid-1980s owing to the collapse of world tin prices (Prunier, 1997, p. 84). Coffee export receipts declined from $144 million in 1985 to $30 million in 1993 (André and Platteau, 1998, p. 3). Hence, export revenues declined, government budgets were cut, and the only remaining source of enrichment was foreign aid. Those who could benefit from it had to be in positions of political power (Prunier, 1997, p. 84). Consequently, elite Hutu engaged in a fierce competition for control of the rapidly shrinking economy.

The 1990-92 war with the RPF contributed further to the devastation of Rwanda's economy. It displaced thousands of farmers in the north, thereby causing reductions in food and coffee production. It closed Rwanda's main land route to Mombasa and the outside world. It destroyed Rwanda's small tourism industry, which had become the third major foreign exchange earner (Vassal-Adams, 1994, pp. 13, 23). But, rather than negotiate in earnest with the RPF, Habyarimana chose to increase the size of his armed forces (from 5,000 in 1990 to 30,000 in 1992), thereby diverting scarce resources from needed food imports, health care, and education.

The rule of dominant persons does not depend on political or economic power alone, but on persuading the ruled to accept an ideology that justifies the rulers' privileged positions and convinces the ruled that their best interests are being protected (Magnarella, 1993, pp. 8-12). 'Ideas and myths can kill, and their manipulation by elite leaders for their own material benefit does not change the fact that in order to operate they first have to be implanted in the souls of men' (Prunier, 1997, pp. 40).

From the 1960s till 1994, the ideology promoted by the Hutu ruling elite was as follows: Tutsi were foreign invaders, who 'could not really be considered as citizens. ... The Hutu had been the "native peasants," enslaved by the aristocratic invaders: they were now the only legitimate inhabitants of the country. ... A Hutu-controlled government was now not only automatically legitimate but also ontologically democratic' (Prunier, 1997, p. 80). This political ideology validated both the persecution of Tutsi and the autocratic rule by some elite Hutu.

As for its economic ideology, the government promoted the idea that the Hutu 'holy way of life' was farming. It strictly limited rural migration to the city. People could not change their residences without government permission, and that was rarely given (Prunier, 1997, p. 77). 'The myth reigned supreme that Rwanda had its own way to go and this way was largely inspired by agrarian and paternalistic values based on the continuation of tradition, food self-sufficiency and the simplicity of rural life (immune from the corruption of modern cities)' (André and Platteau, 1998, p. 5).

Consequently, the government made no attempt to significantly diversify the economy so as to create a viable non-agricultural sector or to limit population growth (except by killing and expelling Tutsi). Religious ideology also contributed to the country's deepening demographic problems. The majority of Rwanda's population was Catholic. Despite Rwanda's evident overpopulation, those in the church and government hierarchy not only refused to promote birth control programs, they actively opposed them. 'Radical Catholic pro-life commandos raided pharmacies to destroy condoms with the approval of the Ministry of the Interior' (Prunier, 1997, p. 89). Evaluating Rwanda's pro-natal policy and almost exclusive agro-economic strategy, the economists André and Platteau write: 'The fact that so few people understood that the path followed by Rwanda was a blind alley still remains something of a mystery' (1998. p. 5).

One of the reasons why political slaughter could be organized along fairly systematic lines was the existence of a culture of obedience. 'Rwandese political tradition, going back to the [19th century] Banyiginya kingdom through the German and Belgian colonial periods, is one of systematic, centralized and unconditional obedience to authority. President Habyarimana was,...the direct inheritor of the *abami* [kings] of old. Most people were illiterate. Given their authoritarian tradition, they tended to believe what the authorities told them' (Prunier, 1997, pp. 141-143). The authorities told them that the Tutsi RPF and all those who sided with them were demons who had to be eliminated. In addition to relieving fear of supposed Tutsi evil, eliminating the demons also earned material rewards (land, cattle, loot) for the killers. Prunier (1997, pp.

141, n. 24) contrasts the Rwandan with the Somali authority culture and concludes that the latter was 'too individualistic to enable such a systematic slaughter to be organized among civilians.'

Conclusion

In short, the sine qua non of the Rwandan genocide was the increasing imbalance in land, food, and people that led to malnutrition, hunger, periodic famine, and fierce competition for land to farm. Rwanda's leaders chose to respond to these conditions by eliminating the Tutsi portion of the population. They employed the weapons of indoctrination to convince the Hutu masses that this strategy was right. However, they failed to employ the kinds of demographic and economic policies that would have addressed these problems in a peaceful and more effective way. These policies would have included birth control, economic diversification into non-agrarian sectors, requests for significant foreign food aid, sincere negotiation with the RPF, and attempts at a regional solution to the refugee problem.

A 1999 United Nations report concluded that the UN Secretariat and Security Council failed to act decisively to prevent or end the 1994 genocide in Rwanda.[3] The report does not, however, accuse these bodies of causing the genocide. I believe their roles had little impact on the conditions endemic to Rwanda that were primarily responsible for the periodic massacres and great tragedy of 1994.

Notes

1. For an excellent discussion of various assassination theories, see Prunier, 1997, pp. 213-229. Two of the best books covering the events of 1994 in detail are Des Forges (1999) and African Rights (1995a).
2. Here I do not argue that Rwanda's relatively large and dense population was the cause of the genocide, only that it was an important contributing factor. For a full rejection of the population argument, see 'The Overpopulation Myth' (African Rights, 1995a, pp. 15-18), where the authors seem to argue, unconvincingly, that overpopulation was nothing more than a myth promoted by President Habyarimana.
3. Independent Inquiry into the Actions of the United Nations during the 1994 Genocide in Rwanda, United Nations, 16 Dec. 1999. Available at www.un.org.

2 The International Role

International Economic Assistance

During the 1950s and early 1980s The World Bank, multilateral agencies, and bilateral donors regarded Rwanda as an economic success when compared to other African countries. With the help of economic aid and a strong market for its coffee exports, Rwanda's gross national product rose steadily. Still, it remained one of the world's poorest countries. By the late 1980s, Rwanda's economy began to deteriorate rapidly. A population growth rate of about three per cent, a decline in coffee prices, severe drought, and government corruption contributed to the decline.

From 1987 to 1992, gross official assistance from foreign countries ranged from a low of $147.1 million (1987) to a high of $241.7 million (1992). In the order of magnitude of their aid, the top assisting countries were Belgium, Germany, France, Japan, Switzerland, and Canada (Sellstrom & Wohlgemuth, 1996, p. 73). The major multilateral sources of grants and loans were: the European Union, the World Bank, the African Development Bank, and the UN Development Programme (*Ibid.*).

In one of the more provocative studies to come out of the Rwandan crisis, Peter Uvin (1998) investigates the relationship between this development aid and the catastrophe of 1994. He believes that *development*, as it was conceptualized, managed, and implemented, contributed to the many processes that culminated in the genocide. Uvin is careful not to condemn development workers and agencies, or cry 'international conspiracy.' His argument is more structural. He maintains that the structure and processes of internationally funded development interacted with the indigenous 'forces of exclusion, inequality, pauperization, racism, and oppression that laid the groundwork for the 1994 genocide' (*Ibid.*, p. 3).

International Efforts for Peace

In 1990 and 1991, representatives of the Rwandan government met with representatives of the Organization of African Unity (OAU), Tanzania, Zaire, and Uganda in an effort to address the region's refugee crisis and Rwanda's internal situation. In August 1992, the OAU and Tanzania coordinated a peace negotiating meeting in Arusha between the Rwandan government and the RPF. As a result of that meeting, the parties signed a protocol on the rule of law (18 Aug. 1992), two protocols on power-sharing (30 Oct. 1992 and 9 Jan. 1993), and a protocol on the repatriation of refugees and the resettlement of displaced persons (9 June 1993) (DPI, 1996, p. 16).

In January 1992, in response to calls by various Rwandan human rights organizations, an International Commission of Inquiry into the human rights violations committed in Rwanda since 1 October 1990 conducted an on-site investigation. The Commission concluded that government soldiers, officials, and mobs headed by government officials had committed widespread human rights abuses (*Ibid.*, p. 20).

In April, the UN special rapporteur on the question of extrajudicial, summary or arbitrary executions conducted an inquiry in Rwanda. His report of 11 August 1993 stated that massacres of civilian populations by FAR and civilians had occurred since 1990. He also reported that 'a climate of mistrust and terror currently prevails in Rwanda,' and that 'although a majority of the population consider that it is possible for the two main ethnic groups to live together peacefully, there is a certain elite which, in order to cling to power, is continuing to fuel ethnic hatred, for instance by spreading rumors prejudicial to the Tutsi' (DPI, 1996, pp. 204-205). The rapporteur also noted that the rapid expansion of the Rwandan Army (FAR) resulted in many undisciplined men being armed. Crimes committed by FAR included 'endemic raping of Tutsi women...looting, armed attacks, revenge killings and murders of civilians, both within and outside the combat zones' (*Ibid.*, p. 206).

On 8 February 1993, the RPF launched a military attack in the Ruhengeri-Gisenyi region of northern Rwanda, in violation of the N'sele cease-fire agreement that Rwanda and the RPF had agreed to in March 1991 after months of negotiations. The RPF maintained that it launched its offensive because the Rwandan government repeated violated human rights and massacred 300 Tutsi in the northwest the previous month. The fighting suspended the Arusha talks and increased the number of internally displaced persons to about 900,000. In April, the UN Department of Humanitarian Affairs and other UN agencies appealed for $78 million to aid displaced Rwandans. By December 1993, UN member states had donated $30.8 million.

At meetings arranged by Tanzania and the OAU in Dar es Salaam in February and March, Rwanda and the RPF agreed to a cease-fire and a resumption of the Arusha peace talks. The RPF also agreed to pull back to its pre-February 8 positions under the supervision of the OAU's Neutral Military Observer Group (NMOG).

The parties resumed the Arusha peace talks in mid-March 1993 and concluded them on 3 August 1993 with the signing of two final protocols, one dealing with the integration of the armed forces and another calling for the ratification of international human rights conventions and the deletion of references to ethnicity in official documents. The Arusha Accord also called on the UN to play a support role during a 22-month transition period towards a fully integrated government and military in Rwanda.

On 5 October 1993 the UN Security Council unanimously agreed to establish the UN Assistance Mission for Rwanda (UNAMIR) (Res. 872/1993). It was to incorporate the OAU's NMOG and to have a four-phase deployment schedule, beginning with a force of 1,428 troops and reaching a high of 2,217 troops and 331 military observers. Its purpose was generally to provide Rwanda with a stabilizing presence and to help facilitate the peaceful implementation of the Arusha Accords. UNAMIR's mission included monitoring the northern demilitarized zone (DMZ), assisting in providing security in and around Kigali and the country, and helping to coordinate humanitarian missions.

By late December 1993, UNAMIR had a force of 1,260 in Rwanda. During the previous month some sixty civilians had been killed near the town of Ruhengeri. UNAMIR observers reported that 'a well-armed and reportedly ruthless group was operating in the area, with a view to disrupting or even derailing the peace process' (DPI, 1996, p. 28).

The Months Leading Up to April

On 11 January 1993, Canadian General Romeo Dallaire, Force Commander of UNAMIR in Kigali, sent an urgent fax to the Peace Keeping Office at UN Headquarters in New York (UNHQ). In his communication Dallaire explained that a Rwandan informant, a former member of President Habyarimana's security staff, was being paid by the president's political party to compile lists of Tutsi and to train the Interahamwe to kill them (Gourevitch, 1998b). The informant explained that the Hutu Power group's plan was to provoke a civil war and to kill some Belgian members of UNAMIR so that Belgium would immediately withdraw its contingent, which was the best armed of the UNAMIR forces. The informant also said that Habyarimana did not have full control over all elements of his old party. The informant disagreed with the plan of Tutsi extermination and wanted protection for his family and himself. Dallaire asked for permission to raid arms caches in Kigali within thirty-six hours. He wanted UNAMIR to become pro-active to prevent the impending exterminations.

At the time, Kofi Annan was Under-Secretary-General for Peace Keeping Operations at UNHQ. His deputy, Iqbal Riza, sent the response. He instructed Dallaire not to act militarily. According to then UN Secretary-General Boutros Boutros-Ghali,

> Guidance was sent [on 11 Jan. 1963] from the Department of Peace-keeping Operations (DPKO) in New York to my Special Representative [Jacques-Roger Booh-Booh of Cameroon] and to the UNAMIR Force Commander. UNAMIR was instructed to contact the President of Rwanda and representatives of three Western [US, French, and Belgian] embassies, two among them permanent members of the Security Council, and to provide the information that had been received concerning a plan to kill Tutsis and the existence of arms caches. ... In response to a suggestion by the Force Commander that UNAMIR mount a military operation, using overwhelming force, to address the issue of the weapons caches, DPKO informed UNAMIR headquarters that such action went beyond the UNAMIR mandate. (DPI, 1996, 31-32)

About Dallaire's urgent message, the Secretary-General also wrote that 'such situations and alarming reports from the field, though considered with the utmost seriousness by United Nations officials, are not uncommon within the context of peace-keeping operations' (*Ibid.*, p. 31).

The next day, 12 January, UNAMIR passed the information on to President Habyarimana and to the American, French, and Belgian Embassies. Consequently, UNHQ, two permanent members of the UN Security Council, and Belgium knew or should have known about the impending holocaust three months in advance.

Iqbal Riza later told Gourevitch (1998b) that any notion of UN intervention at that time would have been unrealistic. Only four months before, eighteen American soldiers had been killed on a UN mission in Somalia. The U.S. was not ready for another mission in Africa. In 1998, a French parliamentary inquiry in Paris would blame the United Nations for failing to avert the Rwandan genocide and would charge that the United States bore special responsibility for resisting demands to boost the UN monitoring force (AP, 1998). While on his eight-nation African tour in May 1998, Kofi Annan, now

UN Secretary-General, told reporters that if he had had one reinforced brigade, he could have saved hundreds of thousands of lives in Rwanda. He blamed UN members for refusing to provide the support needed by General Dallaire (*Ottawa Citizen*, 1998). In 1998 U.S. President Bill Clinton and Secretary of State Madeleine Albright apologized to Rwanda for their country's failure to act promptly during the fatal days of 1994.

On 7 February 1994, when it was already apparent that a transition government and transitional institutions were not being created, the Secretary-General's Special Representative convened a series of consultations involving all political parties at UNAMIR headquarters in Kigali. Although verbal consensus was reached on a number of issues, no positive action followed. Target dates for the creation of a transitional National Assembly came and went. UNAMIR continued in its security and stabilizing role. By late March 1994, its troop strength numbered 2,539 with major contributions coming from Bangladesh (942), Belgium (440), Ghana (843), the Congo (26), Senegal (35), Tunisia (61), Uruguay (25), and Zimbabwe (29). Smaller numbers of troops were contributed by Austria, Botswana, Brazil, Canada, Egypt, Fiji, Hungary, Malawi, Mali, The Netherlands, Nigeria, Poland, Romania, the Russian Federation, Slovakia, and Togo (DPI, 1998, p. 35).

On 14 March 1994 the Belgian foreign minister sent Boutros-Ghali a letter in which he noted the deadlock preventing the formation of a broad-based transnational government. He warned that 'the Rwandese army appears to be increasingly annoyed by the parties' procrastinations, while information on the stockpiling of weapons by the various militias is becoming even more compelling. ...the current political deadlock could result in an irreversible explosion of violence' (DPI, 1998, p. 244).

In addition to the political strain, there was hunger throughout the land. Drought and massive population displacements had markedly reduced agricultural production. In February, the UN Food and Agricultural Organization and the World Food Programme reported that food supplies were critically low everywhere in Rwanda.

6 April and Its Aftermath

On 6 April President Habyarimana's plane was downed by a missile. All aboard were killed. UNAMIR troops attempted to investigate the crash site, but the Presidential Guard denied them access. Throughout the ensuing period of violence, UNAMIR attempted to provide what protection it could for civilians and moderate politicians. General Dallaire ordered a ten-man contingent of Belgian troops to protect Rwandan Prime Minister Agathe Uwilingiyimana. When the ten arrived at her home, they were confronted by the Presidential Guard, who commanded them to lay down their weapons. To show their peaceful intent, they did so. Once unarmed, they were hacked to death by a mob. The episode caused shock in Belgium.

The Secretary-General advised the Security Council that the evacuation of foreign nationals, UN civilian staff, and aid workers from Rwanda was urgently needed, but it would require UNAMIR to have two or three more battalions to do the job. On 12 April 1994, the Belgian Foreign Minister informed the Secretary-General that Belgium had decided to immediately withdraw its contingent of over 400 troops from UNAMIR. These, the best equipped of the UNAMIR troops, had vital communications equipment and heavy weaponry. The Secretary-General asked Belgium to at least leave the weaponry for UNAMIR's use. Shortly thereafter, however, the Belgium contingent left, weapons and all, and Brussels advised the Security Council to suspend UNAMIR operations completely. Another prediction by Dallaire's informant regrettably came true. Many Belgian soldiers reportedly wanted to stay and work to stop the killing (Des Forges, 1999, p. 620). Later, at the International Criminal Tribunal for Rwanda, Belgian Lieutenant Luc Lemaire testified that if Belgium had been more courageous his contingent could have saved many people (ICTR-96-3-I).

With the departure of the Belgian contingent, UNAMIR was reduced to a poorly equipped force of 1,515 with 190 military observers. Then the sizable, but largely ineffective, Bangladeshi contingent also withdrew. Most of the foreign humanitarian workers also departed. Some heroic members of Doctors without Borders and the International Committee of the Red Cross stayed and, along with some brave members of UNAMIR, saved lives. UNAMIR, however, was now short of men, medical supplies, ammunition, fuel, drinking water, and reliable armored personnel carriers. Reportedly, Boutros-Ghali had an assistant telephone Dallaire to pressure him into advocating UNAMIR's total withdrawal (Des Forges, 1999, p. 621). Dallaire refused. Instead, he asked for the means to do more.

Part of UNAMIR's mandate was to protect politicians, but within a week or two after the plane downing, practically all of them had been killed or had fled. UNAMIR was able to save the lives of only a limited number of the civilians who ran to UNAMIR posts seeking protection. Reportedly, some Tutsi asked the UN troops to shoot them before the machete wielding militias got them. While both the OAU and UNAMIR tried in vain to get FAR and RPF to agree to a cease-fire, even if they had succeeded, a cease-fire would not have stopped the Interahamwe and civilian mobs who were slaughtering people with machetes, spiked clubs, hoes, and other hand implements.

The Secretary-General presented the Security Council with three options. The first called for a massive reinforcement of UNAMIR with a new mandate to coerce the opposing forces into a cease-fire. The second would reduce UNAMIR to 270 personnel, who would act as intermediaries between the two sides and continue to try for a cease-fire. The third was a complete UNAMIR withdrawal. On 21 April, the Security Council choose the second, feeble, option. African countries and human rights organizations deplored the decision.

Over the next several weeks, the situation worsened. Finally, on 17 May the Security Council voted to create an UNAMIR II with as many as 5,500 troops. Its mandate included establishing and maintaining secure humanitarian areas and providing security and support for the distribution of humanitarian relief supplies. However, UN member states were not forthcoming with troops and equipment. Consequently, by July, the troop strength of UNAMIR II stood at a mere 503.

On 20 June France requested Security Council approval for a joint humanitarian mission with Senegal to begin immediately. Although human rights NGOs had been encouraging the French government to do something in Rwanda, President Francois Mitterrand decided to act after President Nelson Mandela of South Africa talked about intervening. Paris did not want another representative of the 'Anglo-Saxon world' meddling in France's zone of influence (Prunier, 1997, p. 281). France was also opposed to the English-speaking RPF, who might topple Rwanda's French-speaking Hutu government.

The Security Council approved the mission two days later (Res. 929/1994), invoking Chapter VII of the UN Charter and authorizing 'a multinational operation for Humanitarian purposes in Rwanda until UNAMIR is brought up to strength' (DPI, 1996, pp. 308-309). By invoking Chapter VII and adding the words 'all necessary means' to the resolution, the Security Council authorized the French-Senegalese mission to use military force to establish secure conditions for its humanitarian objectives.[1] This was the kind of mandate that General Dallaire had sought and was denied back on 11 January and repeatedly in April.

By early July, the French-led mission, known as 'Operation Turquoise,' consisted of 2,330 French and 32 Senegalese troops, stationed just over the Rwandan border in Zaire at Goma and Bukavu. They were later joined by troops from Chad (44), Guinea-Bissau (35), Mauritania (10), and Egypt (7). The mission established a protection zone for displaced persons in the Cyangugu-Kibuye-Gikongoro triangle in south-western Rwanda. Some observers charge that France, which had been a regular supplier of military training and arms to the Habyarimana regime, used Operation Turquoise to bring in ammunition for FAR and ultimately allowed FAR, the Presidential Guard, and Hutu militias to escape into Zaire through the protective triangle (Des Forges, 1999).

In another version of this contested history, retired General Christian Quesnot, who had served as head of President Francois Mitterrand's personal military staff in 1994, told a 1998 French parliamentary commission that when 3,000 French troops stepped in unilaterally in June, it was solely on a humanitarian basis. 'We have been accused of many things, but I want to say that journalists and NGOs and intellectuals do not have a monopoly on compassion' (*Toronto Star*, 1998). 'We tried at the time [to raise another international force not linked to the UN to halt the massacres] and spoke to the Belgians and the Italians. Moreover, the Americans had three hundred marines next door in Burundi,' Quesnot said. 'France could not intervene alone because we would have been again accused of stepping in to prevent the victory of the Rwandan Popular Front. But the Belgians wanted to leave and the Americans did not want to step in after losing men in Somalia. If they had known there would be a genocide, I'm sure they would have stepped in' (*Ibid.*).

By 25 July 1994 UNAMIR II had fewer than 500 of its authorized 5,500 troops in Rwanda. African countries had volunteered 3,000 more, but they lacked necessary equipment and transportation. By early October, after the French withdrawal, UNAMIR II consisted of 4,270 troops, mostly deployed in safe zones where they provided security and assistance to humanitarian relief operations.

The Refugee Crisis

Approximately 1.5 million Hutu, mostly civilian refugees, fled into Zaire in July. Their flight constituted one of the largest and most abrupt refugee movements in history. It also created an immense humanitarian crisis. Cholera and dysentery rapidly spread throughout refugee camps that lacked sufficient food, drinking water, and medicine. The UN Rwanda Emergency Office (UNREO) coordinated a major humanitarian relief effort involving the Department of Humanitarian Affairs, the Food and Agricultural Organization, the UN Children's Fund, the UN Development Programme, the Office of the High Commissioner for Refugees (UNHCR), the World Food Programme (WFP), and the World Health Organization (DPI, 1996, pp. 371-382). In addition, by

September 98, NGOs, including the International Committee of the Red Cross and the Red Crescent Societies, were also providing vital contributions (*Ibid.*).

During the period from April to December 1994, the international community allocated about $1.4 billion of assistance to Rwanda.[2] The European Union and the United States accounted for about 50 per cent of this total. About half of the $1.4 billion was expended by or channeled through UN agencies, especially UNHCR and WFP. The money channeled through these agencies went to NGO implementing partners, with the Red Cross receiving 17 per cent of the total (Eriksson, 1996, p. 25).

Addressing Human Rights Violations

In accordance with UN resolutions, René Degni-Ségui, the Special Rapporteur on Human Rights, visited Rwanda in June and July 1994. He concluded that genocide of Tutsi, assassination of moderate Hutu, and other massive and serious violations of human rights had occurred. He also called for the establishment of an international tribunal to bring the guilty to justice (DPI, 1996, p. 570). In response to Degni-Ségui's report, the Security Council requested the Secretary-General to establish as a matter of urgency 'a Commission of Experts to examine information on grave violations of international humanitarian law and possible acts of genocide in Rwanda' (S/Res/935-1994). On 26 July 1994, the Secretary-General appointed Mr. Atsu-Koffi of Togo, Ms. Habi Dieng of Guinea, and Mr. Salifou Fomba of Mali to serve as the Special Commission.

The Commission visited Rwanda and neighboring countries in August and September 1994. It met with government officials, conducted investigations, and received information from the Special Rapporteur on Human Rights, the UN High Commissioner for Refugees, the OAU, NGOs, and private individuals. The Commission concluded that there had indeed been a concerted plan by Hutu elements motivated by ethnic hatred to exterminate Tutsi. It recommended that the Security Council amend the 1993 statute that created the International Criminal Tribunal for the Former Yugoslavia so that those responsible for genocide and other grave crimes in Rwanda could be brought to justice before that Tribunal (DPI, 1996, pp. 345-361). On 8 November 1994 the Security Council adopted Resolution 955 by which it established an independent international criminal tribunal for Rwanda.

Dallaire's Demons

One of the sad and controversial foreign figures to be spawned by the Rwandan crisis is Canadian General and UNAMIR Force Commander Romeo Dallaire. Rwanda was Dallaire's first senior UN peacekeeping command and his first exposure to Africa. Despite this lack of experience, he firmly believed hell would ignite in Rwanda, and he wanted UN authorization and military power to prevent it. Once Rwanda erupted, Dallaire bravely did the best he could to save lives with his small, underequipped contingent. Of Dallaire, African Rights (1995a, p. 1114) writes:

> After 6 April, UNAMIR almost totally failed in Rwanda. Its only redeeming feature was the personal reputation of its Canadian commander, General Romeo Dallaire. Though survivors of the genocide cannot forgive him for UNAMIR's lack of political will to end the slaughter of civilians, Dallaire is regarded as tough, forthright and courageous. He struggled to do what he could, and frankly admitted his difficulties. But his seniors refused to do what was necessary.

Upon his return home, Canada awarded Dallaire the Meritorious Service Cross for his work in Rwanda. In 1997, however, the Belgian Senate concluded that Dallaire had been unprofessional and indifferent to the plight of the soldiers. Relatives of some of the ten Belgian soldiers murdered in Rwanda have publicly blamed the Canadian for their loss. And, at a French parliamentary inquiry in 1998, General Christian Quesnot criticized Dallaire for not disobeying orders in order to curb the 1994 genocide. Quesnot, who had served as head of former president Francois Mitterrand's personal military staff in 1994, said the 2,500 men in UNAMIR commanded by 'Monsieur Dallaire' could have halted the massacres which were then limited to Kigali. Quesnot's reference to Dallaire as 'Monsieur' (Mister) rather than by his military rank reportedly was said with contempt (*Toronto Star*, 1998).

The Canadian Defense Department has stood by Dallaire, rejecting the Belgian allegations and promoting him to three-star general. However, Dallaire himself has suffered from post-traumatic stress disorder. The General once told an interviewer he burst into tears in a supermarket because the smell of fresh fruit reminded him of Rwanda. Dallaire acknowledges that the horror of Rwanda has caused him to lose his sense of humor. It took two years, he says, for the full impact of his experiences to hit him. He simply could not 'keep it in the drawer' any longer. 'I became suicidal because there was no...there was no other solution. I couldn't live with the pain and the sounds and the smell. Sometimes, I wish I'd lost a leg instead of having all those grey cells screwed up' (Blanchfield, 1998). He took an extended leave of absence for mental health reasons, and has undergone therapy to help him recognize and control the triggers that bring back the demons of Rwanda.

In 1998, General Dallaire was called to Arusha to testify at the International Criminal Tribunal for Rwanda as an expert witness in the Akayesu trial (see Chapter 7). Once again he wept as he told of the horrors he was unable to prevent.

Shortly before this book went to press, a United Nations special investigative committee, headed by former Swedish prime minister Ingvar Carlsson, issued a strongly worded report accusing the UN Secretariat, the UN Security Council and Belgium of responsibility for failing to prevent or end the genocide in Rwanda in 1994.[3] The report, commissioned by Secretary General Kofi Annan, who was then head of the peacekeeping department, blames Annan and his predecessor, Secretary General Boutros Boutros-Ghali, of equivocal decisions in the face of impending disaster. It also concludes that the United States administration—represented at the United Nations by Madeleine K. Albright—diminished the seriousness of the problem in Rwanda and negatively influenced that body's interest in acting more decisively. The report determined that the UN ignored warnings of the impending genocide, especially those coming from General Romeo A. Dallaire.

Notes

1. On only five previous occasions has the Security Council authorized member states to use military force under Chapter VII. Those involved missions to defend the Republic of Korea (1950), to intercept tankers transporting oil to Southern Rhodesia (1966), to expel Iraq from Kuwait (1990 and 1991), and to provide humanitarian relief in Somalia (1992-1993) (DPI, 1996, pp. 54).
2. For a brief, excellent report on the international response to the genocide, see Mackintosh (1995).
3. Independent Inquiry into the Actions of the United Nations during the 1994 Genocide in Rwanda, United Nations, 16 Dec. 1999, available at www.un.org.

3 Expanding the Frontiers of Humanitarian Law: The International Tribunal for Rwanda

Faced with one of the most appalling cases of genocide that the world had witnessed since World War II, the UN Security Council, having just created an international criminal tribunal for humanitarian law violators in the European states of the former Yugoslavia, decided it could do no less for African Rwanda. Since the Rwandan conflict was internal rather than international, the statute for its tribunal complements rather than replicates that of its Yugoslavian counterpart. Because the statute for the Rwandan Tribunal contains a number of legal innovations, it will contribute significantly to the development of the humanitarian law of internal armed conflict. This chapter analyzes these innovations. It also discusses the creation of the tribunal, its substantive and procedural law, as well as its initial activity.

The genocide campaign following Habyarimana's death ended in July 1994 when the RPF Army routed the Hutu militias and army. The RPF and moderate Hutu political parties formed a new government on 18 July 1994, but the country was in chaos. The government pledged to implement the Arusha Peace Accords on power sharing previously reached by Habyarimana's regime and the RPF on 3 August 1993. The prime minister reportedly stated that his government might prosecute and execute over 30,000 Hutu for murder, genocide, and other crimes committed during Rwanda's holocaust (Burkhalter, 1994). The U.S. government, fearing that such a prospect would amount to a new cycle of retribution and keep Hutu refugees from returning home, sent John Shattuck, U.S. Assistant Secretary of State for Human Rights, to Kigali to encourage the government to delay its plans for prosecution in favor of judicial action by an international tribunal.

Creating the Tribunal

On 1 July 1994, the UN Security Council adopted resolution 935 in which it requested the Secretary General to establish a commission of experts to determine whether serious breaches (including genocide) of humanitarian law had been committed in Rwanda (UN Doc. S/935/1994). In the fall of 1994 the commission reported to the Security Council that genocide and systematic, widespread, and flagrant violations of international humanitarian law had been committed in Rwanda, resulting in massive loss of life (UN Doc. S/1994/1125). On 8 November 1994, the UN Secretary-General submitted to the Security Council a statute for the International Criminal Tribunal for Rwanda (hereafter, ICTR or Tribunal), stating that he was 'convinced' that 'the prosecution of persons responsible for serious violations of international humanitarian law [in Rwanda]...would contribute to the process of national reconciliation and to the restoration and maintenance of peace' (UN Doc. S/Res/955, 1994, hereinafter, statute).[1] He recommended that this Tribunal, like the tribunal created by the Security Council in 1993 for the former Yugoslavia, be established under Chapter VII of the United Nations Charter.[2] Given the urgency of the situation, the Secretary-General did not involve the General Assembly in the drafting or review of the statute. Subsequently, however, the General Assembly passed its own resolution welcoming the Tribunal's establishment (UN Doc. A/Res/49/206, 1994).

The Security Council adopted the Secretary-General's report and the resolution sponsored by the United States and New Zealand by a vote of thirteen to one, with China abstaining. Ironically, Rwanda was the only Security Council member to vote no (Preston, 1994). Rwanda expressed three objections. It wanted the statute to contain a provision for capital punishment. It also preferred that the temporal jurisdiction of the Tribunal extend back to 1990 to cover earlier crimes, and it wanted the Tribunal to be based in Rwanda itself. The statute as accepted by the Security Council does not allow for capital punishment and limits its temporal jurisdiction to the year 1994 only. Subsequently, the Security Council decided to locate the Tribunal in Arusha, Tanzania. Furthermore, the Security Council rejected Kigali's proposal that Rwandan judges sit on the Tribunal.

Initially, Rwandan President Bizimungu publicly criticized the Security Council vote saying it would only lead to a 'secret' court that would 'exonerate' the true organizers of the genocide. Later, however, a Rwandan spokesperson said his government would cooperate fully with the UN court (Thomas, 1994). Rwanda's only realistic hope of bringing the major instigators of the genocide to justice is through the Tribunal. Most of those chiefly responsible had fled the country, and Rwanda lacks the political leverage, the necessary extradition treaties, and the resources necessary to gain custody and to try them (see Marie, 1995).

One of the most innovative and expeditious recommendations in the Security-General's report was that of establishing the Tribunal through the exercise of the Security Council's powers under Chapter VII of the UN Charter. As Antonio Cassese, the first president of the International Criminal Tribunal for the Former Yugoslavia (ICTY), explained, 'the traditional approach of establishing such a body by treaty was discarded as being too slow (possibly taking many years to reach full ratification) and insufficiently effective as Member States could not be forced to ratify such a treaty against their wishes' (UN Doc. S/1994/1007, 29 Aug. 1994).

By going the Chapter VII route, the Security Council obliged all UN member states to cooperate with the Tribunal and to honor any lawful requests it makes for assistance under the ICTR statute. Specifically, Articles 39, 41, and 48 of Chapter VII of the UN Charter provide the legal basis for the Security Council's establishment of the Tribunal. Article 39 states that the Security Council shall determine when threats to peace exist, and shall, in accordance with Articles 41 and 42, determine what measures shall be taken to maintain or restore international peace and security. (Presumably, the Security Council regarded the massive flow of refugees and remnants of the Hutu militias to neighboring countries as a threat to international peace.)

While Article 42 addresses military actions, Article 41 provides that '[t]he Security Council may decide what measures not involving the use of armed force are to be employed to give effect to its decisions, and it may call upon the Members of the United Nations to apply such measures.' The article goes on to list the kinds of actions (e.g., interruptions of economic and communication ties) that these measures 'may include.' Although Article 41 does not include judicial measures in its list expressly, it does not preclude them, and the use of the phase 'may include' denotes that the list is not exhaustive.

Article 48 obligates UN member states to support the Security Council's decision by cooperating in its implementation. The article provides that '[t]he action required to carry out the decisions of the Security Council for the maintenance of international peace and security shall be taken by all Members of the United Nations or by some of them, as the Security Council may determine.'

Composition of the Tribunal

The ICTR originally consisted of two trial chambers (with three judges each) located in Arusha, an appeals chamber (with five judges) located in The Hague, The Netherlands, the office of the prosecutor located in Kigali, and a registry located in Arusha. In January 1995, the UN appointed Honore Rakotomanana, the former president of the Supreme Court of Madagascar, as deputy chief prosecutor for the Tribunal. He worked out of an office in Kigali under the supervision of Richard Goldstone, chief prosecutor for both the ICTR and the ICTY, whose office was located in The Hague. (Canadian judge Louise Arbour replaced Goldstone in October 1996.)

In June 1995, the six trial judges and five appeals judges took their oaths and held their first plenary session in The Hague. All were elected and appointed by the United Nations. The six original trial judges were Lennart Aspegren of Sweden, Laity Kama of Senegal, Tafazzal Hossain Khan of Bangladesh, Yakov Arkadievich Ostrovsky of Russia, Navanethem Pillay of South Africa, and William Hussein Sekule of Tanzania. They elected Judge Laity Kama as the ICTR's first president. The Rwanda Tribunal shares the appeals chamber that had already been created for the ICTY. That chamber initially included Justices Antonio Cassese of Italy, Haopei Li of China, Gabrielle Kirk McDonald of the United States, Ninian Stephen of Australia, and Datuk Wira Lal Vohrah of Malaysia.

The Tribunal's first registrar and chief administrative officer was Andronido Adede, a Kenyan attorney, who has served as Deputy Director of the Codification Division in the UN Office of Legal Affairs. The Registrar's Office is responsible for judicial administration and also for all the management and diplomatic support required by the Tribunal. These responsibilities include support and protection for witnesses and victims, the operation of a detention center, and the organization of legal assistance for the accused, as well as the management of personnel, finances, and security. The two official languages of the Tribunal are English and French, but witnesses at trials may also testify in Kinyarwanda, the native language of Rwanda. The registrar is responsible for necessary translators and translation services.

The Tribunal's Jurisdiction

Article 1 of the Tribunal's statute limits the ICTR's temporal jurisdiction to the year 1994 only. That article also states that the ICTR 'shall have the power to prosecute persons responsible for serious violations of international humanitarian law committed in the territory of Rwanda and Rwandan citizens responsible for such violations committed in the territory of neighboring states.' Consequently, the statute gives the Tribunal both personal and territorial jurisdiction in Rwanda as well as limited personal and territorial jurisdiction in surrounding states. By contrast, the statute of the ICTY grants that Tribunal jurisdiction 'in the territory of the former Yugoslavia' only (Art. 1).

By granting the ICTR the competence to prosecute Rwandans who allegedly committed certain crimes abroad, the Security Council has added a new dimension to the humanitarian law of noninternational armed conflict. Rwanda formally requested the establishment of a tribunal, thereby voluntarily surrendering some of its jurisdiction to the Security Council's judicial creation. By contrast, according to the statute, Rwanda's neighbors must surrender some of their jurisdiction to the Tribunal without choice. All states have the authority or competence to prosecute Rwandans for crimes committed on their territories. However, because the Tribunal by its statute has primacy over the national courts of all states [Art. 8(2)], it may formally request that any neighboring state's court defer certain cases to its competence. This request carries with it the threat of a penalty for noncompliance. Should any state notified of a deferral request not respond satisfactorily within 60 days, 'the [Tribunal's] Trial Chamber may request the President to report the matter to the Security Council,[3] which presumably will consider sanctions. Requiring states to surrender to a UN Security Council creation their competence to prosecute persons for criminal acts committed on their own territories is another novel use of UN Charter Chapter VII. Surrounding states, such as Zaire and Kenya, have protested this demand on their sovereignty. State action and reaction, claims and responses will determine whether this kind of measure, taken by the Security Council under Chapter VII, will become an accepted principle of international law to be applied again in the future.

Subject Matter Jurisdiction

Because the Security Council is not a legislative body, it had no competency to enact substantive law for the Tribunal. Instead, it authorized the Tribunal to apply existing international humanitarian law applicable to noninternational armed conflict. The humanitarian law included in the Tribunal's statute consists of the Genocide Convention,[4] (ratified by Rwanda), crimes against humanity (as defined by the Nuremberg Charter),[5] Article 3 Common to the Geneva Conventions,[6] and Additional Protocol II[7] (also ratified by Rwanda). Both the prohibition and punishment of acts of genocide and crimes against humanity are part of customary international law imposing legal obligations on all states (McCoubrey, 1990, p. 140).

Article 2 of the statute replicates Articles 2 and 3 of the Genocide Convention. Statute Article 2(2) defines genocide as any of the following acts committed with intent to destroy, in whole or in part, a national, ethnical, racial, or religious group; killing group members; causing serious bodily or mental harm to group members; deliberately inflicting on the group conditions calculated to bring about its complete or partial physical destruction; imposing measures intended to prevent birth within the group; and forcibly transferring children to another group. Persons who commit genocide or who attempt, conspire, or incite others to commit genocide are punishable.

Similar to the Geneva Conventions, the Genocide Convention (Article 5) obligates state parties to enact the legislation necessary to provide effective penalties for persons guilty of genocide. Article 6 of the Genocide Convention also requires that persons charged with genocide be tried in the territory where the act was committed, 'or by such international penal tribunal as may have jurisdiction with respect to those Contracting Parties which shall have accepted its jurisdiction.' Consequently, the surrounding states of Zaire and Tanzania, as ratifying parties to the Genocide Convention, undertake to charge persons responsible for genocide in Rwanda and to extradite them for prosecution either back to Rwanda or to a competent international tribunal that they recognize. Since the Geneva Convention's entrance into force in 1951, the only international tribunals competent to prosecute those accused of genocide in limited geographic areas have been the ones established by the Security Council for the former Yugoslavia and Rwanda. By virtue of Chapter VII obligations under the UN Charter, all UN members (including Burundi, Uganda, and Kenya, which had not ratified the Genocide Convention) are required to recognize these Tribunals and surrender suspects to them if requested to do so. Non-UN members, however, can decide for themselves whether they wish to recognize these international tribunals for purposes of surrendering suspects.

Obligations to prevent and punish acts of genocide are not confined merely to the 107 states that had ratified the Genocide Convention as of 1 January 1994. Because the prevention and punishment of genocide have become part of international customary law, the International Court of Justice has noted that 'the principles underlying the [Genocide] Convention are principles which are recognized by civilized nations as binding on states, even without any conventional ratification.[8]

Statute Article 3, 'Crimes against Humanity,' follows Article 6(c) of the Nuremberg Charter. It empowers the Tribunal to prosecute persons responsible for the following crimes when committed as part of a widespread and systematic attack against any civilian population on national, political, ethnic, racial, or religious grounds: murder, extermination, enslavement, deportation, imprisonment, torture, rape, persecutions on political, racial, and religious grounds, and other inhumane acts.

Employing the Nuremberg concept of crimes against humanity in Rwanda constitutes an important legal development. The Nuremberg Charter was established to prosecute 'war criminals,' and it explicitly defined crimes against humanity as specified inhumane acts committed 'before or during the war.' Traditionally, war was defined as a state of armed conflict between two or more states (Oppenheim, 1952), but legal experts have debated about the legal criteria of war, for example, whether a formal declaration of war is required, whether there can be domestic war, whether the parties must be recognized states, and the like.

Some legalists may now wonder whether applying the Nuremberg Charter to Rwanda's internal conflict is appropriate. Although the charter is explicitly included in the statute for the ICTY, that conflict involved more than one state, and consequently meets the war criterion of the charter. The statute for the Rwandan Tribunal characterizes the situation there as an internal armed conflict. Hence, it does not include the 'grave breaches' sections of the 1949 Geneva Conventions, which apply to international armed conflict and are regarded as customary international law. By containing the Nuremberg concept of crimes against humanity in its statute, the Rwandan Tribunal represents an important extension of international humanitarian law to internal conflicts. The UN Security Council, the Tribunal's creator, ignored the ambiguity of the war concept and with its authoritative voice has made crimes against humanity an internal as well as an international offense of customary international law.

Article 4 of the statute empowers the Tribunal to prosecute persons committing or ordering to be committed serious violations of Article 3 common to the four Geneva Conventions of 1949 and of the Additional Protocol II thereto of 1977. These violations include: a) violence to life, health, and physical or mental well-being of persons, in particular murder, torture, or mutilation; b) collective punishments; c) taking of hostages; d) acts of terrorism; e) outrages upon personal dignity, in particular humiliating and degrading treatment, rape, enforced prostitution, and any form of indecent assault; f) pillage; g) sentences or executions rendered extra-judicially or without due process; and h) threats to commit any of the foregoing acts.

Neither Article 3 Common nor Protocol II applies to conflicts of an international nature. Rwanda's neighbors–Burundi, Tanzania, Uganda, and Zaire (but not Kenya)–had ratified both the Geneva Conventions and Protocol

II. However, unlike the grave breaches sections of the Geneva Conventions, Article 3 Common and Protocol II do not require ratifying parties to criminalize the above acts or to prosecute or extradite alleged violators either to the state on whose territory their acts occurred or to a competent international tribunal. As noted above, each UN member state is obligated under Chapter VII of the UN Charter to cooperate with Security Council measures taken to maintain international peace.

Article 28 of the Rwandan Tribunal's statute specifies that states shall cooperate with the Tribunal and comply without undue delay with any request for assistance, including the arrest or detention of persons and the surrender of suspects to the Tribunal. Consequently, the UN Security Council, through its creation of this Tribunal, has added a compulsory arrest and surrender requirement to acts that the Geneva Conventions and Protocol II had previously conceptualized as being governed by domestic discretion. This represents another important extension of humanitarian law.

The Security Council's and the General-Secretary's decision that the Tribunal should have jurisdiction over natural persons and not juridical persons, such as associations, is reflected in statute Article 5. Accordingly, membership alone in a criminal organization would not be sufficient to subject someone to the Tribunal's jurisdiction. Article 6 addresses 'individual criminal responsibility.' It states that any person who planned, instigated, ordered, committed, or aided and abetted in the planning, preparation, or execution of any crime mentioned in Articles 2 to 4 of the statute shall be individually responsible for the crime. An accused's official position, even as president or prime minister, shall not relieve him of responsibility or mitigate punishment. The doctrine of individual responsibility for violations of humanitarian law was emphasized in the post-World War II Nuremberg and Tokyo trials (Lupis, 1987, pp. 353-354). It was also codified in the Geneva Conventions of 1949.

Furthermore, in accordance with the humanitarian law principle of 'command responsibility,' superiors are criminally responsible for the criminal acts of their subordinates if they knew of the acts and did not take reasonably necessary measures to prevent or stop them. Although following a superior's orders will not relieve subordinates of criminal responsibility, it may mitigate their punishment if the Tribunal determines that justice so requires.

Concurrent Jurisdiction and Tribunal Primacy

Given the magnitude of the crimes committed in Rwanda, the successful prosecution of all those responsible would greatly exceed the resource capacity of the Tribunal. One Africanist estimated that the number of Rwandans directly involved in the acts of killing amounted to between 75,000-150,000 (Jefremovas, 1995, p. 28). Statute Article 8(1) states that '[t]he International Tribunal for Rwanda and national courts shall have concurrent jurisdiction to prosecute persons for serious violations of international humanitarian law committed in the territory of Rwanda and Rwandan citizens for such violations committed in the territory of neighboring States, ...' However, the statute goes on to state that the Tribunal 'shall have primacy over national courts of all States,' such that it may formally request national courts to defer to its competence [Article 8(2)].

To respect the principle of *non-bis-in-idem* (not twice for the same) and to avoid the potential for double jeopardy, statute Article 9 states that no person tried by the Tribunal shall be retried by a national court for the same acts. However, persons already tried by a national court for crimes covered by Articles 2 to 4 of the statute may be retried by the ICTR if the litigated acts had been characterized as ordinary crimes, the case was not diligently prosecuted, or the national court proceedings were neither impartial nor independent or were designed to shield the accused from international responsibility.

Rules of Procedure

The ICTR's Rules of Procedure are based on those of the Tribunal for the Former Yugoslavia. They incorporate the fundamental due process guarantees to a fair and speedy trial found in Article 14 of the International Covenant on Civil and Political Rights (ICCPR). Consequently, this Tribunal, like its counterpart for the former Yugoslavia, will become a medium whereby international human rights standards will have significant influences on the development of international criminal law. Its due process guarantees include: the right to the presumption of innocence (Rule 62); the right against self-incrimination (Rule 63); the right to counsel of choice or to free legal assistance if indigent (Rule 42); the right to inspect the prosecution's incriminating and exculpatory evidence (Rules 66-68); the right to privileged communication with counsel (Rule 97); the right to public proceedings (Rule 78); the right to challenge the prosecution's evidence and to present evidence in one's defense (Rule 85); and the right of appeal (Rule 108).

Only the prosecutor or his duly delegated deputy may commence a proceeding by submitting an indictment supported by evidence to a designated Tribunal judge for confirmation (Rule 47). Neither victims, states, nor NGOs may initiate proceedings before the Tribunal.

Once a Tribunal judge confirms an indictment, he or she may issue arrest and search warrants (Rules 54-55). The Tribunal's registrar transmits the arrest warrant to the national authorities of the state having jurisdiction over the accused 'together with instructions that at the time of the arrest the indictment and statement of the rights of the accused be read to him in a language he understands... .' (Rule 55). The arresting state authorities shall notify the registrar and arrange to transfer the accused to the seat of the Tribunal where the president will arrange for his detention (Rules 57 & 64) in a UN-supervised detention center in Arusha, Tanzania.

If the notified state authorities have been unable to arrest the accused, and if the registrar has, at the prosecutor's request, published notices of the arrest warrant in widely circulated newspapers, a trial chamber may, after finding the prosecutor's evidence sufficient, issue an international arrest warrant that shall be transmitted to all states (Rule 61). The president of the Tribunal has the authority to notify the Security Council of any state that refuses to honor the Tribunal's arrest warrant or that impedes the execution of such a warrant (Rule 61-E).

Soon after his arrest, the accused is brought before a trial chamber and formally charged (Rule 62). The trial chamber shall satisfy itself that the accused's right to counsel is respected and that he understands the indictment (Rule 62). It shall call on the accused to enter a plea, and should the accused fall silent, it shall enter a plea of not guilty on his behalf (Rule 62). The trial chamber then instructs the registrar to set a date for trial (Rule 62). There are no provisions for trials in absentia.

In deference to the Second Optional Protocol to the ICCPR of 1989, the Tribunal is not authorized to impose the death penalty. This, however, leads to an ironic situation. Owing to its limited resources, the Tribunal is expected to go after what prosecutor Goldstone called the 'big fish' and try at most twenty persons a year. Consequently, those chiefly responsible for the genocide would receive, if convicted by the Tribunal, a sentence of years, up to life, whereas lesser figures tried and convicted in Rwandan courts could be sentenced to death.

Tribunal Indictments

Approximately one year after the genocide the Tribunal reportedly had a list of four hundred suspects as a result of ongoing investigations (AP, 1995). Most of these were officials and military leaders of the former Hutu-dominated regime who had fled to other countries.

As noted above, all states are obligated to cooperate with the Tribunal. Such cooperation includes arresting and extraditing to it suspects and indicted persons. However, Kenyan President Daniel arap Moi stated that he not only would not cooperate with the Tribunal, he would prevent it from seeking out suspects in his country (Lorch, 1995). Moi had been a close friend of Rwandan President Habyarimana. Consequently, many high-ranking Rwandan Hutu officials found refuge in Kenya in 1994. According to human rights officials, some Kenyans have financially benefited from these wealthy Rwandans from the former government (Tunbridge, 1995).

Immediately after Moi's remarks, Chief Prosecutor Goldstone sent him a letter, asking for clarification and warning that Kenya's refusal to cooperate with the Tribunal would be regarded as a breach of Kenya's obligations under international law, a matter for the Security Council to consider (Goldstone, 1995). President Moi soon retracted his statement (AFP, 1995), but human rights watchers doubted his sincerity.

In December 1995 ICTR Judge Navanethem Pillay publicly stated that certain African states, particularly Zaire and Kenya, were hampering ICTR efforts to bring criminals to justice (Crossette, 1995). Some observers believed that the presidents of Zaire and Kenya were more concerned about the regional balance of power than about crimes against humanity. They supported Rwanda's former rulers because they regarded the successor RPF-led government as a client of Uganda's President Yoweri Museveni, their rival for leadership in East and Central Africa (Hilsum, 1995). If any African state refuses to cooperate with the Tribunal, as required under the UN Charter, it may become a sanctuary for some suspected criminals, but it may also be sanctioned by the UN Security Council. Possible sanctions could include a moratorium on international economic aid, something no African country can afford to lose.

The work of the ICTR had initially been slowed by a lack of facilities in Arusha and by UN budgetary constraints.[9] Finally, on 12 December 1995, the Tribunal issued its first indictments against eight Hutu, charging them with genocide and crimes against humanity. The Tribunal kept their names and whereabouts secret so as to facilitate their arrests. On 10 January 1996, Prosecutor Goldstone asked Belgium to extradite three formerly high ranking Hutu to the Tribunal, which had designated them as suspects. Belgian authorities promised to do so after their parliament passed the necessary enabling legislation. Later, on 19 February 1996, the Tribunal indicted two formerly high-ranking Hutu being held in a Zambian jail. Zambian authorities agreed to extradite. More indictments were forthcoming.

More Recent Developments

When it began, the ICTR did not have a courtroom facility or a detention center. Construction on both was not completed until well into 1996. A second courtroom became operational in September 1997, so that two trials could be conducted simultaneously. On 30 April 1998 the Security Council amended the ICTR statute so as to permit the election of a third three-judge trial chamber (Res. 1165, see Appendix B). It also approved of the construction of a third courtroom. The UN elected judges Lloyd Williams of Jamaica, Dionysios Kondylis of Greece and Pavel Dolenc of Slovenia as members of the third chamber in November 1999 (AN, 1999a). However, when Judge Dionysios Kondylis resigned before ever assuming his position at court, Secretary-General Kofi Annan appointed Judge Asoka de Zoysa Gunawardena of Sri Lanka to take his place (AN, 1999b). Construction on the third courtroom was completed in April 1999.

Members of the ICTR were quite aware that, with over thirty people in custody and with more coming, steps must be taken to speed up the trial process. The judges have modified the rules of procedure, hoping to make trials more efficient, and the prosecution is considering proposals for joint trials of up to five people together. The disposition of cases should accelerate as more guilty pleas are entered. Two of the first three cases ended with such pleas. Those changes, combined with the three streams of trials now possible, should quicken the adjudication process.

As of March 1999, there were thirty-six indictees being held in detention. Of these, thirty were in ICTR's detention center in Arusha; one was in Texas fighting extradition (Magnarella, 1998), and two who had pleaded guilty were being detained in secret safe-houses for security purposes. The majority of the thirty-six detainees had held positions of responsibility in Rwanda and had allegedly incited or directed others to take part in the genocide. They include seven former ministers, eight senior civil servants, six military officers, four political leaders, three militia leaders, three senior figures in the 'media of hate,' two businessmen, a priest, and a doctor. All were arrested outside Rwanda and surrendered by government authorities to the ICTR. Twelve were sent from Kenya; six from Cameroon; three from Zambia; two each from Belgium, Benin, Ivory Coast, and Togo; and one each from South Africa, Burkina-Faso, Mali, and Namibia. One suspect surrendered himself to the Tribunal before being arrested. Ten other people have been indicted, but not yet taken into custody.

A serious problem facing the Tribunal was where to imprison convicted persons. The ICTR statute provides that 'imprisonment shall be served in

Rwanda or any of the States which had indicated to the Security Council their willingness to accept convicted persons.' By the end of 1998 Austria, Belgium, Denmark, Norway, Sweden, and Switzerland had expressed their willingness to receive convicts in their national prisons. No African country had declared its readiness to do the same. The UN Secretary-General and the ICTR would prefer for 'sociocultural reasons' that those convicted by the Tribunal serve their sentences in African countries. In early 1999, Mali signed an agreement with the Tribunal to assist with imprisonment. Negotiations with other African countries were on-going. The reluctance of African states to offer prison space can be attributed to their inability to meet the high level of prison standards expected by the UN.

Apprehending Theoneste Bagosora

Probably the 'biggest catch' among those being held is Colonel Theoneste Bagosora, called the mastermind of the genocide. He had assumed de facto control of military and political affairs in Rwanda after President Habyarimana's death. Bagosora was arrested in Cameroon under an international arrest warrant issued by Belgium in connection with the murder of ten Belgian UN peacekeepers in April 1994. Rwanda also requested his extradition. A Cameroon court ruled that the ICTR had priority over Belgium for purposes of extradition, but did not rule on the Rwandan request. In July 1996, Belgium dropped its request for extradition in deference to the ICTR and to statute Article 8(2), which addresses concurrent jurisdiction and ICTR primacy. Still, there was a delay in turning over Bagosora.

Andronico Adede, the ICTR's first registrar, complained that he made frequent trips to Cameroon in connection with Bagosora's surrender without result. In October 1996, he said he had waited three days for an audience with Cameroon's justice minister, but did not get one. A senior justice official in Cameroon told Reuters that he was trying to impress his superiors with the importance of surrendering Bagosora to the Tribunal. 'Even officials of the United States Embassy came to see me yesterday. They are very interested in the case,' he confided (Noubissie, 1996). The official said that he reminded his superiors that if Cameroon did not surrender Bagosora within sixty days after receiving the ICTR's request, it risked being sanctioned by the United Nations (*Ibid.*). In January 1997, Cameroon complied by sending four suspects, including Bagosora, to Arusha.

The other suspects arrested in Cameroon and surrendered to the ICTR at its request were: André Ntagerura, Minister of Transport and Communications,

Colonel Anatole Nsengiyumva, a former military intelligence chief and alleged death squad member, and Ferinand Nahimana, a founder of Radio Television Milles Collines, which had been used to incite the genocide. Chief Prosecutor Louise Arbour said the four were the first indictees taken into custody by the ICTR who were very influential or held positions of national authority during the 1994 genocide (Reuters, 1997). She added that the four's transfer to Arusha 'marks a capital turning point for the International Tribunal and demonstrates the Tribunal's capability to prosecute the principal perpetrators' (*Ibid.*).

The First Cases and Trials

The ICTR's first completed trial, that of Jean-Paul Akayesu, former *bourgmestre* (mayor) of Taba, opened on 9 January 1997 and closed on 26 March 1998 (see Chapter 7). On 2 September 1998, the Tribunal found Akayesu guilty of genocide and crimes against humanity. A month later he was sentenced to life imprisonment, but both the prosecutor and Akayesu have appealed against this decision. This was an historic trial because it was the first conviction for genocide by an international tribunal, and the first time a court had treated rape as a crime against humanity as well as an act of genocide.

Jean Kambanda, formerly prime minister of the interim government formed in April 1994, was the first person to plead guilty before the Tribunal (see Chapter 6). His plea was accepted on 1 May 1998, and on September 4th he was sentenced to life imprisonment for genocide and crimes against humanity. His voluntary and public acknowledgment of the genocide and his own role in it discredits all those who steadfastly deny that there had even been a genocide. Kambanda agreed to cooperate with the ICTR prosecutor by providing information and evidence against others who are accused. He was sentenced to life imprisonment because of the gravity of his crimes and his failure to show remorse. Kambanda, too, is appealing his sentence.

Omar Serushago, a former militia leader in Gisenyi, also pled guilty. The Tribunal accepted his plea and sentenced him to fifteen years imprisonment. The judges maintained that attenuating circumstances allowed them to show clemency. These included Serushago's guilty plea, his cooperation with the prosecutor, and the assistance he had given to some whose lives were threatened. Unlike Kambanda, Serushago publicly expressed his remorse and called for national reconciliation. He has appealed his sentence on the grounds that it would have been less severe if he had been tried in Rwanda under that country's 1996 genocide law (see Chapter 4).

As of March 1999, ICTR proceedings were at various stages for several other defendants, including: Clément Kayishema, former *préfet* (town official) in Kibuye; Obed Ruzindana, a Kibuye businessman; Georges Rutaganda, vice-president of the Interahamwe militia; and Alfred Musema, former director of a tea-producing factory.

The ICTR and Rwanda

From the beginning, Rwandan authorities were not enthusiastic about the ICTR statute and its location in Tanzania. The Rwandan government has complained that the ICTR unfairly competed with it for suspects arrested in third countries (e.g., Cameroon, Zambia) at Rwanda's request, but then transferred to Arusha at the ICTR's insistence. During the first few years, Rwanda regarded the ICTR as an ineffective expense. This image improved with the appointment of a new deputy prosecutor and the arrest in Kenya in July 1997 of some of those held chiefly responsible for the genocide. In 1998 the Rwandan Ministry of Defense opened its files to the ICTR, and the government began allowing defense witnesses in Rwanda to go to Arusha to testify. It also gave ICTR investigators access to Rwandan court files.

Even by 1998, people in Rwanda still knew too little about ICTR activities, although the Tribunal's Press and Information Office had improved its methods of disseminating information. Initiatives by private media organizations, such as Intermédia and the Fondation Hirondelle, which are dedicated to informing Rwandan citizens about the Tribunal, have had some positive impact.

Conclusion

The ICTR and its predecessor, the ICTY, represent the first attempts by the international community to create international judicial organs to enforce the Geneva Conventions, the Genocide Convention, and laws proscribing crimes against humanity. The Rwandan Tribunal is unique in that it is the first international court to apply crimes against humanity to a non-international conflict and to enforce Article 3 Common and Protocol II of the Geneva Conventions. The extension of its territorial jurisdiction to states not party to the Rwandan conflict represents another new development in international law.

The exact impact that the ICTR will have on the application of international humanitarian law and the legal prerogatives of the UN Security Council acting under Chapter VII of the UN Charter will be determined by actual political and judicial experience, the reactions of states, and the ability of the Tribunal to gain custody over and prosecute a significant number of major criminals. Both Tribunals will influence the way many states view the causes of grave humanitarian crimes and possible strategies for achieving peace and national reconciliation.

The mass murders in Rwanda and the former Yugoslavia did not arise spontaneously. They were instigated by persons in positions of power who sought to gain personal advantages through violent and hideous means. Unless these persons are made to account for their crimes against humanity, the reconciliation necessary for the reconstruction of these torn societies may not be possible. By assigning guilt to the leader-instigators, the Tribunals may also lift the burden of collective guilt that settles on societies whose leaders have directed or ordered such terrible violence. The assignment of guilt by neutral Tribunals may also enable the international community to differentiate between victims and aggressors. It may help erase the belief that interethnic conflicts are genetically inbred and therefore insoluble.

The success of the Tribunals is essential if future crimes against humanity are to be prevented. If human rights can be massively violated with impunity in Rwanda and the former Yugoslavia, we can expect new Hitlers to crop up wherever political advantages can conceivably be gained by committing crimes against humanity. Should the Tribunals not accomplish their main prosecutorial objectives, their creation will still have a lasting effect on the application of humanitarian law to both international and domestic conflicts. They also will have accomplished, as Prosecutor Goldstone has stated, the significant task of putting international humanitarian law and human rights squarely on the international agenda.

Notes

1. The full name of the Tribunal is the International Criminal Tribunal for the Prosecution of Persons Responsible for Genocide and Other Serious Violations of International Humanitarian Law Committed in the Territory of Rwanda and Rwandan Citizens Responsible for Genocide and Other Such Violations Committed in the Territory of Neighbouring States, between 1 January 1994 and 31 December 1994. Resolution 955 and the Statute are reproduced in Appendix A of this book.
2. Works on the International Tribunal for the Former Yugoslavia include: Bassiouni (1995), Magnarella (1995), Meron, (1994), Scharf (1997), and Wedgwood (1994).
3. ICTR Rules of Procedure and Evidence. Adopted on 29 June 1995.
4. Convention on the Prevention and Punishment of the Crime of Genocide. Dec. 9, 1948. U.N.T.S. 277, (hereinafter, Genocide Convention).

5. Charter of the International Military Tribunal. Done at London, Aug. 8, 1945. 59 Stat. 1544, 82 U.N.T.S. 279.
6. Geneva Conventions No. 1-4, Aug. 12, 1949, 75 UNTS 31, 85, 135, 287.
7. Protocol Additional to the Geneva Conventions of 12 Aug. 1949, and Relating to the Protection of Victims of Non-International Armed Conflict, Dec. 12, 1977, 1125 UNTS 609, (hereinafter, Protocol II).
8. *Advisory Opinion on Reservations to the Convention on the Prevention and Punishment of the Crime of Genocide,* 1951 I.C.J. 15.
9. The ICTR's budget was approximately $40 million in 1996, $35 million for 1997, and almost $50 million for 1998. The budget for 1999 was increased to $73 million, to enable the creation of some 250 supplementary posts. As of March 1999, ICTR had a staff of 582. Somewhat more than $5 million has also been allocated for defense attorneys and other defense related activities (ICG, 1999).

4 Criticism and Controversy

Establishing an international tribunal from scratch is a major challenge even under the best of conditions. Organizers of the UN Tribunal for the Former Yugoslavia discovered this even though their tribunal is located in The Hague, The Netherlands–a modern city with all of the necessary communications, building, utilities, and library infrastructure. By contrast, the UN decided to locate the Rwandan Tribunal in the small, undeveloped, and remote town of Arusha, Tanzania, where communications services and electric utilities are quite unreliable, and available office space is limited and spartan. The ICTR occupies part of the Kilimanjaro wing of a three-building complex known as the International Conference Center in Arusha. It is a modest, cement-walled facility built by the Chinese in the 1970s.

In his February 1995 report recommending Arusha to the Security Council, the Secretary-General noted that the Security Council had expressed preference for an 'African seat' (S/1995/134). The Secretary-General recommended against Kigali because it lacked appropriate facilities and posed 'serious security risks in bringing into the country leaders of the previous regime alleged to have committed acts of genocide to stand trial before the International Tribunal.' He noted that Kenya was not receptive to having the Tribunal in Nairobi, but Tanzania would offer facilities in Arusha for little or no rent. He maintained that the proximity of Arusha to Rwanda would facilitate the transportation of witnesses and accused persons between the two. Consequently, for reasons of 'economy and administrative efficiency,' the Secretary-General recommended and the Security Council accepted Arusha as the seat of the ICTR.

In March 1998, however, ICTR Registrar Agwu Ukiwe Okali told a New York audience that the ICTR could not begin practical operations until November 1995, a full year after its creation, 'because there was no logistic infrastructure available for it on the ground in Arusha' (Okali, 1998, p. 6). He went on to say that the UN Security Council had designated this small town in northern Tanzania as the seat 'because of its symbolic significance as the venue of the peace accords signed in August 1993 between the former government of Rwanda and the Rwandan Patriotic Front' (*Ibid.*). Many familiar with the problems of working at the ICTR believe the choice of Arusha was political, rather than practical. They agree that a major African city, such as Nairobi, Kenya, or Dar es Salaam, Tanzania, would have been better choices.

In addition to procuring furniture, computers, telephones, and other basic equipment, ICTR organizers had to recruit personnel for over two hundred positions. Unfortunately, start-up problems were compounded by unqualified and ineffective officials at the highest levels, and worse. Some members of the staff were openly charging racism in hiring, incompetence, and nepotism at the ICTR (Reuters, 1997). These allegations led to a UN investigation.

Paschke Report I

In February 1997, Karl Paschke from the UN Office of Internal Oversight Services submitted his report on the audit and investigation of the ICTR to UN Secretary-General Kofi Annan (UN Doc. A/51/789, 6 Feb. 1997). The following paragraphs have been taken verbatim from his report:

> In response to a request by the General Assembly and following complaints received from staff members and Member States, the Office of Internal Oversight Services (OIOS) conducted an audit and investigation of the International Criminal Tribunal for Rwanda. In reviews of the records of the Tribunal and interviews of present and former staff members, both United Nations-assigned and seconded, OIOS became aware of serious operational deficiencies in the management of the Tribunal. Such deficiencies have developed virtually from its inception and continued through November 1996 when OIOS conducted this review at Kigali, Arusha, United Republic of Tanzania and at United Nations Headquarters.
>
> In the Tribunal's Registry not a single administrative area functioned effectively: Finance had no accounting system and could not produce allotment reports, so that neither the Registry nor United Nations Headquarters had budget expenditure information; lines of authority were not clearly defined; internal controls were weak in all sections; personnel in key positions did not have the required qualifications; there was no property management system; procurement actions largely deviated from United Nations procedures; United Nations rules and regulations were widely disregarded; the Kigali office did not get the administrative support needed, and construction work for the second courtroom had not even started.

The Office of the [Deputy] Prosecutor in Kigali had administrative, leadership and operational problems. Functions were hampered by lack of experienced staff as well as lack of vehicles, computers and other office equipment and supplies. Lawyer posts were vacant and, of the almost 80 investigator posts, only 30 had been filled. Prosecution strategy deficiencies were noted. The witness-related programmes had not been fully developed.

The report recommended appointing a new Deputy Prosecutor 'with substantial leadership skills and relevant experience in the running of a prosecutorial office and directing of significant criminal investigations.' It also described internal friction:

> The relationship between the Registry and the Office of the Prosecutor was often characterized by tension rather than cooperation. The Registrar has asserted that his function as Chief Administrative Officer of the Tribunal gave him ultimate authority for all matters having administrative or financial implications.
>
> The effective establishment of the Tribunal had been affected by the short-term funding arrangements, by the geographical separation of the [Deputy] Prosecutor's Office [in Kigali, Rwanda] from the other organs of the Tribunal [in Arusha, Tanzania and The Hague, Netherlands] and by the lack of adequate infrastructure at both Arusha and Kigali.
>
> These difficulties were exacerbated by the recruitment of inexperienced or otherwise unqualified staff, decisions for which both the Registrar and the Secretariat bear responsibility. OIOS acknowledges that the less than attractive financial conditions at Arusha and Kigali did not facilitate the recruitment of qualified staff. The Secretariat also failed to provide adequate short-term support by assigning qualified staff members temporarily to the Tribunal especially during the critical start-up phase.

The report went on to note that:

> The difficulties in the Registry were compounded by the absences of the Registrar [Andronico Adede of Kenya], who spent more than 150 days on official travel during the period from December 1995 to October 1996. This means more than five months, or half of his time on duty, had been spent travelling. Within a period of one and a half months the Registrar travelled for 32 days. One reason for his long and frequent absences is that the Registrar believed that in many cases he should personally deliver warrants of arrest or negotiate and arrange the transport of individuals in custody. The absence of the Registrar was

made more critical by the departure in mid-1996 of the Deputy Registrar, who has not been replaced.

The report further stated that:

> The Deputy Prosecutor [Honore Rakotomanana of Madagascar] reports that his relationship [with the Registrar] has often been 'strained and testy' and that 'the Registrar has never failed to remind us of his pre-eminence rather than his readiness to carry out the mission which has brought all of us together.'

With respect to security of ICTR staff in Kigali, the report maintained that,

> Participants and victims and their families and friends who survived the events of 1994 still live in Kigali. The tensions that led to crimes that caused the creation of the Tribunal remain part of the fabric of the city. The anger of some of the populace against UNAMIR [UN Assistance Mission to Rwanda] has been transferred in part to the Tribunal, which is now housed in UNAMIR's old offices in the Amahoro Hotel. Threats were received regularly; three Tribunal investigators were assaulted; a bounty was placed on United States citizens.

The report was also critical of witness-related programs:

> The slow development of witness-related programmes hampered trial preparation and has the potential to impact negatively on the trials. The Tribunal's Witness Protection Programme, under the auspices of the Registry, was developed only recently and without the involvement of any person with specialized training and relevant experience. Critically, the programme did not include any post-trial phases. The Registrar advised OIOS that an agreement was being concluded with a non-governmental organization knowledgeable in this area to assist the Tribunal. The Witness Clothing Programme had not been developed. Many of the witnesses, in the cases for which indictments have been confirmed, live in rural areas and will require assistance in securing appropriate clothing and shoes. Less than $5,000 had been allocated.

Finally, the report acknowledged the difficult task of creating an international tribunal from scratch and the insufficient level of support from the UN Secretariat:

> Thus struggling with the daunting tasks of establishing the Registry, securing staff, and constructing a courtroom, offices and prison facilities, the Registrar

was given little active help by the Secretariat departments. To his credit, the Registrar has accomplished these tasks in a difficult environment.

In his cover letter accompanying the report to the General Assembly, Secretary-General Kofi Annan noted that:

> The Secretary-General is committed to closing the gap identified by the Office of Internal Oversight Services and taking all required measures to streamline and strengthen the Secretariat's support to the Tribunal. In immediate follow-up to the interim recommendations of the Office of Internal Oversight Services, additional assistance is currently being provided to the Tribunal on site and a more consistent pattern of support is being developed to meet its needs.

Soon after this report became public, Annan received the resignations of Registrar Adede and Deputy Prosecutor Rakotomanana and replaced them with Agwu Ukiwe Okali of Nigeria and Bernard Acho Muna of Cameroon. Okali, a lawyer, had joined the UN Office of Legal Affairs in 1975 and had worked on diverse legal matters. Muna had previously served in Cameroon as a prosecutor and a magistrate.

Rwanda's Indictment

At the end of February, the Rwandan government issued its own indictment of the ICTR at the UN and over Radio Rwanda in Kigali (BBC, 1997). The government complained that the ICTR's structure and function were fundamentally flawed; it needed remedial measures in four major areas:

1) Organization. Because the Chief Prosecutor is located in The Hague at the ICTY, he/she devotes great attention to that Tribunal and little to the ICTR. The ICTR needs its own independent prosecutor, not a deputy prosecutor, who reports to the Hague.

2) Personnel. Too many ICTR staff members are unqualified or inexperienced.

3) Prosecution and investigation strategy. The ICTR has failed to investigate the perpetrators of the genocide who continue their illegal activities in refugee camps outside of Rwanda. Thus far, it has indicted small fry, rather than big fish. The ICTR has failed to carry out investigations in prefectures, such as Cyangugu (southwestern Rwanda). Although it cites security reasons for these failures, it has failed to solicit the assistance of the Rwandan government in providing security.

4) Misconceptualization of purpose. Some senior officials, such as Chief Prosecutor Louise Arbour, have misconceptualized the role and mandate of the Tribunal. They are more concerned with history's view of themselves and the development of jurisprudence rather than with the prosecution of criminals. According to the Rwandan government, she has issued instructions to prosecution attorneys never to oppose applications for adjournment of proceedings although the defendants' efforts at procrastination are evident and well documented. Her policies 'are at variance with the spirit of [UN] resolution 995/94 which seeks to promote national reconciliation and maintenance of peace in Rwanda by bringing to justice perpetrators of genocide and other serious violations of international humanitarian laws.'

The Arusha correspondent for the *East African* newspaper claimed that Kigali was demanding two separate Tribunals (Kibanga, 1997). In her March 1997 article, the corespondent maintained that the Rwandan government believed UN Secretary-General Kofi Annan should have sacked Chief Prosecutor Louise Arbour along with Registrar Adede and Deputy Prosecutor Honore Rakotomanana.

The ICTR was clearly on the defensive and needed to polish its image in Rwanda and the world. In June 1997 and again in July 1998, Agwu Okali, ICTR's new registrar, made official visits to Kigali to improve relations with the Rwandan government. During his first visit, he called at the offices of the Ministry for Foreign Affairs, the Director of the Cabinet, the President of the Republic, the Ministry for Women and Social Affairs, the Ministry of Justice, the Chief Prosecutor of the Rwandan Supreme Court, and the Information Directorate. Registrar Okali also visited an important genocide site and the newly established Nelson Mandela village for widows and orphans of the genocide (ICTR/INFO-9-2-056).

On his second visit, Okali met with Major General Paul Kagame, the most powerful man in Rwanda. Kagame, a Tutsi, held the positions of Vice-President and Minister of Defense in the new Rwandan government. He had led the RPF to victory in 1994. Okali briefed Kagame on the work of the ICTR and the case of former premier Jean Kambanda. The ICTR's public information office expressed elation with the visit. In its press release, the office said that Vice-President Kagame expressed his 'pleasure at Mr. Okali's visit' and noted that the 'Tribunal had made significant progress in its work under difficult circumstances, and offered any further assistance the Tribunal might require of the Rwandan government' (ICTR/INFO-9-2-133).

An Attorney's Complaint and Paschke Report II

Broad criticism of the ICTR also came from American Michael G. Karnavus (1997), who had served briefly as a defense attorney for Jean-Paul Akayesu. He complained that Registrar Adede had no trial or court experience and lacked concern for the rights of the accused. Unlike the Paschke Report, Karnavus also criticized the judges. He explained that while the Tribunal had adopted the common law adversarial system, the judges came from countries with civil code-accusatorial systems. He charged that 'these judges are unable or unwilling to appreciate the vast differences in the two legal traditions, particularly with respect of the role of the defense attorney.' He complained also that the president of the Tribunal refused to grant him enough time and financial resources to prepare an adequate defense. However, another defense attorney at the ICTR, with whom I spoke, thought Karnavus' criticism of the judges was somewhat exaggerated.

One year later, senior ICTR officials were delighted to see the UN Office of Internal Oversight Services' 6 February 1998 Report (UN Doc. A/52/784). Known as Paschke II, the report stated that 'improvements were observed in virtually every area surveyed by the team of investigators and auditors.' The report noted that new Deputy Prosecutor Muna's leadership had significantly strengthened his Office, and that 'the relationship between the Registry and the other two functions of the Tribunal, the Chambers and the Office of the Prosecutor, is reported by all parties to have improved.' In addition, 'the [UN] Secretariat, notably the Department of Management and the Office of Legal Affairs, has taken necessary and affirmative steps to assist the Tribunal in achieving the goals set by the Security Council.'

Judge Aspegren's Brief

However, just as Tribunal officials were feeling relieved, Lennart Aspegren, one of ICTR's six judges, told a Swedish newspaper in July 1998 he was resigning (APW, 1998a). Aspegren, a 67-year-old Swede, cited mismanagement and incompetent leadership at the Tribunal as the reasons for his departure. He acknowledged the appointment of new registrar, Agwu Okali, but complained that 'all the incompetent people his predecessor hired are still here. Those who accept bribes and embezzled money are promoted. Those who voice criticism are formally cautioned. That is why I am stepping down early.' Judge Aspegren also complained about facilities: 'We don't have a reference library. ... We lack telephones and newspapers. We are completely cut off. We don't even have a website on the Internet so that people can follow our work.[1] Of all useless departments, the information department is the worst.'

Earlier, in May 1998, Judge Aspegren had gone public with similar criticisms (*Monitor*, 1998). At that time he also faulted some prosecutors and defense attorneys, saying they had 'little or no experience with criminal trials.' Registrar Okali was reportedly 'infuriated' by Judge Aspegren's decision to resign in protest over alleged bad management and inadequate working condition. Okali told the press that 'all [Judge Aspegren's] statements are false. These are all sound effects with no factual bases. He's impressed by no one but himself' (APW, 1998b).

In a more judicial tone, ICTR President and Judge Laity Kama of Senegal countered Judge Aspegren's criticisms in an official statement dated 28 July 1998 (ICTR\INFO-9-3-003). While respecting Judge Aspegren's right to air his complaints, Judge Kama, speaking for himself and the other four judges, said that 'we cannot share in all respects the negative opinion [Judge Aspegren] expressed on the ICTR administration.' Judge Kama noted that since the arrival of Registrar Okali in March 1997, 'a spirit of cooperation has prevailed, which has led to appreciable changes in the Judges' working conditions.' He explained that 'a second courtroom has been constructed, which allows the two Trial Chambers to sit simultaneously, courtrooms have been air-conditioned and other necessary facilities have been provided: fax, e-mail, access to legal databases, and the recruitment of a librarian.' He also complimented the Press and Public Affairs Section for its improved efforts. He acknowledged that 'more lawyers must be recruited at higher levels' and the 'construction of a third courtroom must begin without delay.' 'In the quest to solve these problems,' he advised, 'we favour the path of cooperation over the kind of fruitless confrontation which has so poisoned the atmosphere at the ICTR in the past.'

The Ntuyahaga Affair

The case of the itinerant Rwandan army major stirred up controversy both inside the ICTR as well as among the ICTR, Belgium and Rwanda.[2] On 6 June 1998, Bernard Ntuyahaga, a former major in the Rwandan Armed Forces, voluntarily showed up at the ICTR and asked to be held as a 'protected witness.' He had come from Zambia, where he had sought refuge from the RPF back in

1994, but feared for his life there. Shortly after he appeared in Arusha, the Prosecutor's Office (PO) realized that it had a major suspect. Ntuyahaga was formally arrested, and the PO sought an indictment against him on five separate counts connected to the 1994 genocide. Judge Yakov Ostrovsky confirmed the indictment on 29 September 1998, but threw out three of the five counts. The Russian judge dispensed with the counts of genocide and conspiracy to commit genocide, and confirmed only those pertaining to crimes against humanity in connection with the murder of Prime Minister Agathe Uwilingiyimana and ten Belgian UN troops on 7 April 1994. In addition, he ruled that the remaining counts should be collapsed into one single charge of crimes against humanity. According to Deputy Prosecutor Bernard Muna, conviction on such a count would result in a maximum sentence of only five or ten years.

On 25 February 1999, the prosecution filed a motion to have all charges against Ntuyahaga withdrawn. In support of its motion, the PO said its mandate as part of a 'global police aimed at shedding light on the events that occurred in Rwanda in 1994' could not be achieved by proceedings run on the basis of a single count indictment whose factual elements relate only to the murder of the former Prime Minister and the ten Belgian UN troops. The prosecution of isolated criminal acts, which can no longer be placed within the context of conspiracy to commit genocide, does not promote the prosecutorial objective of shedding light on the tragic events that occurred in Rwanda in 1994, the PO maintained. By confirming a single-count indictment, Judge Ostrovsky had 'narrowed the scope of prosecution and has deprived the Prosecutor of the opportunity to execute her strategy of prosecuting Bernard Ntuyahaga for totality of his criminal involvement.'

The PO requested that the ICTR hand Ntuyahaga over to Belgium, noting that Article 8 of the Statute of the ICTR refers to the concurrent jurisdiction of the Tribunal and individual national courts over serious international human rights violations that fall within the ICTR's responsibility. The PO pointed out that Belgium had already begun proceedings against Bernard Ntuyahaga for his alleged involvement in the murder of the ten Belgian UN troops. However, Ntuyahaga's lawyer, Georges Komlave Amegadjie of Togo, opposed the prosecution's motion, arguing there were no provisions in the ICTR statute or rules empowering it to hand over an accused person to national courts if the prosecutor withdrew charges.

In a letter dated 25 February to Tribunal President Judge Laity Kama, the Belgian Justice Minister expressed his government's willingness to support the PO's motion to withdraw the indictment, but with the proviso that the Tribunal then extradite Ntuyahaga to Belgium. Ntuyahaga had been on Brussels' wanted list for a long time. Brussels had secured an international arrest warrant for him as early as 1995. When the Belgian government learned that he was in Tanzania, it presented that state with an application for his extradition, even before the ICTR had begun its proceedings.

Trial Chamber I granted the prosecution leave to withdraw its indictment against Ntuyahaga on 18 March. Then, in a surprise move that shocked the prosecution, Belgium, and Rwanda, the judges ordered Ntuyahaga's immediate release from detention and instructed the registrar to execute that decision 'if need be with the cooperation of the Tanzanian authorities.' Ntuyahaga, still fearing for his life, asked to be returned to the ICTR detention facility in Arusha for protection. He dreaded being sent to Rwanda where he would most probably face the death penalty.

The Belgian government immediately asked the Tribunal to transfer Ntuyahaga to Belgium for trial or to deliver him to Tanzanian authorities for subsequent extradition to Belgium. But the judges ruled they had no power to order either. Brussels also made a written submission to the Tanzanian authorities, saying that under the terms of their bilateral extradition agreement, Tanzania should detain Ntuyahaga without delay and extradite him to Belgium, because it was the first country to file an extradition request (Rwanda had also submitted an extradition request for Ntuyahaga to Tanzania).

The ICTR Registry released Ntuyahaga on 29 March in Dar es Salaam, after the Trial Chamber rejected a defense motion seeking a stay of execution on its decision of 18 March. Registrar Agwu Okali issued Ntuyahaga a Safe Conduct document, requesting that the UN and its member states and international organizations grant safe conduct and cooperation to Ntuyahaga allowing him to travel freely. The registry also gave Ntuyahaga enough money to purchase a plane ticket to return to Zambia. Despite the document, Tanzanian authorities arrested Ntuyahaga the same day for having entered the country illegally.

The ICTR's release of Ntuyahaga provoked a strong diplomatic reaction from both Belgium and Rwanda. The Belgian government threatened to review its cooperation with the Tribunal and also sought an audience with the United Nations Secretary-General on the Tribunal's handling of the case. Rwanda registered its 'shock' and 'disappointment' at the release and accused the ICTR of insensitivity and incompetence.

According to ICTR Deputy Prosecutor Bernard Muna, he and Belgian authorities had been in close contact about the Ntuyahaga case from the beginning. Muna said Rwanda had not, like Belgium, pushed for Ntuyahaga's extradition at an early stage, and had been slow to volunteer much evidence to help the prosecution in Arusha. Muna explained that his office had withdrawn its indictment on the understanding Ntuyahaga would face extradition to Brussels at a later stage. He added that Ntuyahaga had confessed to driving the vehicle that carried the ten Belgian peacekeepers to the military camp where they were hacked to death.

On 31 March, Muna's superior, ICTR Chief Prosecutor Louise Arbour, filed a motion asking the judges of Trial Chamber I to rescind the safe conduct letter on the grounds that it went beyond the statute and rules of the Tribunal. The judges declared the point moot, since Tanzania had attached no significance to the document and had arrested Ntuyahaga. In a declaration on 22 April, however, the judges criticized the registrar's handling of the affair by declaring that the registry had acted *ultra vires* (beyond its power) in issuing the letter of safe conduct to Ntuyahaga.

Kingsley Moghalu, legal advisor to Registrar Okali, told reporters that the registrar had asked the judges for guidance in implementing any decision, but received none. Therefore, he used his own judgment and acted in good faith. At this point, the prosecutors were politely criticizing the judges and the registrar, the judges were criticizing the prosecutors and the registrar, and the registrar was criticizing the judges. As for Belgium and Rwanda, they were criticizing the entire ICTR institution.

In early May, Tanzanian justice officials rejected Belgium's request on grounds that the extradition treaty between the two countries did not provide for extradition to a country other than where the alleged crimes were committed. They would now pursue the Rwandan application for Ntuyahaga's extradition, but it might be several months before a final decision was reached. Disappointed once again, Peter Gijsels, advisor to the Belgian justice minister in Brussels, called the decision a political one. But, he said, Belgium's aim is to see justice done. Belgium would cooperate with Rwanda, if Ntuyahaga were extradited there.

Notes

1. The ICTR currently has a website that can be accessed through the United Nations home page: www.UN.org.
2. This section is based on the following sources: *Ubutabera Independent Newsletters of the ICTR*; Hirondelle, an independent news agency covering the ICTR (available at www.hirondelle.org), and numerous news accounts available in the Lexis News Library under the search word 'Ntuyahaga.'

5 The Situation in Rwanda

As it was successfully routing the Hutu army and various Hutu militias, the RPF Army began rounding up Hutu suspected of participating in the genocide and committing other crimes. The International Committee of the Red Cross (ICRC) claimed that by August 1996, Rwanda had about 80,000 Hutu (mostly followers, rather than leaders) crammed into antiquated, putrid prisons, detained indefinitely while awaiting formal charges. Reportedly, over two thousand had died under these conditions (Reuters, 1995). As Van Lierop (1997, p. 887) notes, however, 'prison conditions may not be so disproportionately harsh when compared with living conditions for the average Rwandan citizen.' Rwanda emerged from the 1994 genocide as a devastated and poor country.

The new justice minister was housed in a building without telephones or windowpanes. He and his team of four did not even have paper or typewriters. Every piece of equipment had disappeared from official buildings, most of which were in ruins. The judicial staff had been reduced to around twenty investigators and a few secretaries and court clerks.

Capable of holding only 12,000 people, the penitentiaries were overloaded by the flood of detainees. The ICRC, UNICEF, and the UN Development Program (with funds from The Netherlands, Belgium, Denmark, Sweden, and Finland) took on the difficult task of improving and expanding existing detention facilities and arranging new, semi-permanent holding centers. Authorities provided women and children with somewhat more privacy and better protection.

Building a Judiciary

Before the imprisoned suspects could be tried, Rwanda had to build a judicial system. As Schabas (1996) explains, the previous Rwandan legal system had been corrupt. In its final years, especially, the Habyarimana regime violated human rights with impunity. Lawyers and judges did not or could not prosecute the numerous atrocities that preceded the 1994 genocide. In 1993 there were about seven hundred judges and magistrates, but fewer than fifty of them had any formal legal training. Until 1995 there was no independent bar association. The pre-genocide government decided who was qualified to act for the defense.

Rwanda's justice system was inherited from Belgium in the 1950s. It was based on Roman-Germanic legal tradition and operated in French. The courts were and still are organized on a pyramid system. The judicial structure calls for 146 local courts (*tribunaux de canton*) at the level of the communes, twelve district courts (*tribunaux depremière instance*) at the level of the prefectures, four appeal courts (*Cours d'appel*) and a Court of Final Appeal (*Cour de cassation*). There was also a separate Security Court, which had jurisdiction over political crimes, but it was abolished in June 1996.

The Public Prosecutor's Office deals with investigations and is organized within a structure paralleling that of the courts. It has twelve regional offices at the level of the prefectures, each composed of a prosecutor, deputies, and judicial police inspectors (*inspecteurs de police judiciaire*). Police inspectors represent the Public Prosecutor's Office at the commune level. Each appellate court has a public prosecutor (ICG, 1999).

As of 1 February 1995, Rwanda had only a few surviving judges and not a single functioning court. The trials of those suspected of involvement in the genocide were repeatedly postponed owing to lack of resources. The magistrates and civil servants associated with the former regime had fled the country. Almost all Tutsi civil servants and magistrates had been killed, along with a large number of their Hutu colleagues who had shown signs of independence under the former regime. Experienced Hutu jurists and lawyers were not trusted. There were almost no trained lawyers among the new arrivals from the diaspora. The few lawyers allied with the RPF had been educated in the common law systems of various east African states, particularly Uganda and Kenya. They were mystified by the complexities of Rwandan criminal law and procedure, which follow the continental model. They were further handicapped by their inability to speak and read French, the language in which Rwandan legislation and most legal commentary were written (Schabas, 1996, p. 533).

The Arusha Accords, signed on 4 August 1993 between the former government and the RPF, contained a number of provisions intended to guarantee judicial independence. Rwanda's new government affirmed its commitment to end the culture of impunity that had reigned for years and to ensure that the genocide would be punished. However, the reconstruction of the judiciary depended largely on contributions from western countries and UN agencies and help from non-governmental organizations (NGOs), such as *Réseau des Citoyens*. While it readily accepted outside donations, the Rwandan government made it clear that it did not want foreigners to work in its judiciary system as judges or prosecutors.

The Organic Law

In August 1996, Rwanda's National Assembly approved the 'Organic Law on the Organization of Prosecutions for Offenses Constituting the Crime of Genocide or Crimes against Humanity'. This law was designed to expedite the trials of the thousands held in prison and to encourage Hutu refugees to return from abroad. The government hoped that once the judiciaries identified and prosecuted those primarily responsible for the genocide, Rwanda's Tutsi would believe justice was being served and would be less likely to seek revenge on returning Hutu refugees. The Organic Law covers offenses committed between 1990 and 1994 (versus only 1994 for the ICTR), so as to deal with the massacres that occurred during the civil war prior to President Habyarimana's death.

The law distinguishes genocide planners and mass murderers from others, and offers reduced prison sentences if they confess. It divides offenders into four categories. The first category includes genocide organizers or planners, persons with military or governmental authority who committed or encouraged genocide, 'notorious murderers who by virtue of the zeal or excessive malice with which they committed atrocities, distinguished themselves in their areas of residence or where they passed,' and persons who committed 'acts of sexual torture' (Schabas, 1996, p. 538). The second category covers ordinary murderers, who do not fall into category one; the third category comprises those who committed other serious crimes against the person; and the fourth category comprises those who committed crimes against property.

The Organic Law also contains a confession and guilty plea procedure that can reduce sentences markedly for offenders in the second, third, and fourth categories. Offenders must give full and detailed descriptions of the offenses to which they confess with information about accomplices, if any. The district prosecutor's office is then required to verify if such confessions are complete and conform to the facts. If the prosecutor decides to accept a confession, the court must respect that decision. Category two murderers found guilty at trial are liable to life imprisonment. If they plead guilty before trial, their sentences will be seven to eleven years. If they plead guilty at trial, their sentences are twelve to fifteen years. The sentence of a category three accused is reduced by one-half of that ordinarily applied to the crime if he/she pleas guilty before trial or by one-third if he/she pleas guilty at trial. Convicted category four defendants receive suspended sentences. In addition, courts will treat property crimes as civil offenses, offering victims the opportunity to sue for damages.

Category one criminals face the death penalty, but they may benefit from the guilty plea procedure, provided their names are not on a list of category one suspects previously published in the *Official Gazette*. In November 1996, The Supreme Court's chief prosecutor had a list of 1,946 category one suspects published in the *Gazette* (Des Forges, 1999, p. 751).

The purposes of the confession procedure are to speed up the prosecution process and reduce the prison population. But during the first year of the Organic Law, fewer than sixty people confessed. After the 24 April 1998 executions of twenty-two persons convicted of genocide, however, the number increased markedly. Less than three months later 'justice officials said the first public executions prompted more than 2,000 to confess to their crimes in exchange for leniency' (AAP Newsfeed, 1998). By the end of 1998, 8,615 people had begun the confession process, but others still refused to do so, citing mistrust of government authorities or fear of reprisals against them and their families (Des Forges, 1999, p. 762).

Within each of the twelve local courts there are one or more special courts set up to deal exclusively with genocide cases. Three judges or lay magistrates, who have each received four months of training, preside over each. The Rwandan criminal justice system is largely based on the inquisitorial procedure, under which judges question witnesses and defendants and make findings of fact. Their role and integrity are therefore crucial to a fair trial. Many magistrates are Tutsi, who may feel under pressure to convict. The prosecutor general attached to the Supreme Court is the overall supervisor of legal proceedings.

Danger for Witnesses

Although the Rwandan government pledged to guarantee the safe return of refugees living abroad in sprawling and unsanitary camps (Kaban, 1995), it was concerned about Hutu extremists waging an insurgency campaign from the camps located in Tanzania and Zaire. There Hutu militias were reportedly forcibly inducting young men into their units and threatening to invade Rwanda to retake power. According to UN observers, from May to June of 1996 Hutu extremists had killed ninety-nine witnesses to the genocide in order to prevent them from testifying before either Rwandan courts or the ICTR (AFP, 1996b). Many of those murdered had lived in Rwanda's Gisenyi province, located just across the Zairian border from Hutu refugee camps. Because there is so little documentary evidence of much of the 1994 killing, prosecutors will have to rely on eyewitness accounts. Hence, the murder of key potential witnesses will hamper the prosecutorial process.

Increasing Legal Personnel

In an urgent attempt to increase the number of judicial personnel, large-scale training programs with one- to five-month courses began in January 1995. The programs usually involved a radio appeal for candidates holding secondary school diplomas, an admission test, training culminating in examinations, and the allocation of posts to those who passed them. Remarkably, candidates of both ethnicities have come forward. Consequently, magistrates sitting in the special genocide courts may be either Hutu or Tutsi. By 1999, 750 police inspectors, 200 deputy prosecutors, 300 magistrates, 150 court clerks, and 150 prosecutor's secretaries had received training (ICG, 1999).

Unfortunately, low salaries, difficult working conditions, and general insecurity have discouraged more people from applying and have caused some officials to abandon their posts. A few magistrates, police inspectors, and deputy prosecutors have themselves been arrested as suspects in the genocide; others have been killed by armed Hutu bands seeking to perpetuate the genocide. On 1 January 1999 the government increased civil service salaries by between 25 per cent and 45 per cent (ICG, 1999). Hopefully, these raises will help correct the situation.

In conjunction with the training courses, a great deal of work has also gone into restoring buildings and providing vehicles and other essential material to the judiciary. Over $4 million, coming mainly from the European Union, Switzerland, Belgium, Japan, and the United States, have been invested in building repairs. Europe, Canada, the UN, and the U.S. also financed programs to supply equipment and vehicles to the Ministry of Justice, the courts, and the prosecutors' offices. These donors have given additional assistance to communal police forces and the gendarmerie (the Rwandan national police force) (ICG, 1999).

The Trials Begin

By January 1997, genocide courts in Kigali, Byumba, Gikongoro, Kibuye, Nyamata, and Kibungo were trying cases and applying the Organic Law. By

20 January, the courts had convicted nine persons (all Hutu) of genocide and had sentenced them to death by firing squad. Among them were a former official of the National Republican Movement for Democracy and Development (Habyarimana's ruling party), three schoolteachers, a hospital aide, a low-level local official, and a Burundian Hutu, reportedly one of many who participated in the genocide (AFP, 1997b).

All those convicted have fifteen days to appeal against their verdicts on the narrow bases of error of law or flagrant error of fact (Des Forges, 1999, p. 752). The trials were generally brief. The first, involving three defendants, lasted only four hours (*NYT*, 1997). During the trial, the 250 courtroom spectators booed the defendants and cheered the prosecutors. Most, if not all, of those convicted could not find lawyers willing to represent them; consequently, they had to defend themselves. These procedures raised serious concerns on the part of the UN High Commissioner for Human Rights and Amnesty International.

On 7 January, Jean Flamme, secretary general of *Avocats sans Frontiéres* (Lawyers without Borders), based in Belgium, announced that three members of his organization would soon go to Kigali to establish a permanent office to carry out a project entitled 'Justice for All in Rwanda' (Fox, 1997). They planned to provide assistance to the Rwandan judiciary and to defend those being tried for genocide. By the end of 1998, about twenty members of *Avocats Sans Frontières* (ASF), mostly African lawyers, were in Rwanda representing defendants under the patronage of the Bar Association's Office of Consultation and Defense. Such lawyers stay and work in Rwanda for between five weeks and one year. ASF wants to maintain a presence of fifteen lawyers at any one time in the hope that 50 per cent of trials are covered. The organization's creation is a brave attempt to use the rule of law as a signal that justice will one day be established in a land almost destroyed by genocide.

British barrister Paul Hardy recently described his experience working with ASF for four months in Rwanda (Hardy, 1999). He and fourteen other ASF lawyers lived together in a house in Kigali. They received briefs on the 'cab-rank' principle and would expect to be in court anywhere in the country three or four days a week. He represented defendants who had been charged with genocide and crimes against humanity. But specific accusations varied widely. He represented some alleged to have planned genocide in a district, others who appeared to have killed with extraordinary zeal, others who were coerced into action, and a fourteen-year-old boy who allegedly used his dogs to chase Tutsi from their hiding places. In light of the low acquittal rate, his efforts were concerned mainly with avoiding the death penalty.

The accused and victims are too numerous for all to benefit from the services of ASF. In early 1999, eighty-eight Rwandans entered a training program organized by the Danish Human Rights Center that will qualify them to provide legal representation for both victims and the accused. The Rwandan government also explored the more conciliatory mechanism of a truth commission. In January 1997, a Rwandan delegation, including the Labor and Social Affairs Minister, went to South Africa to inquire about the policies and operations of that country's truth and reconciliation commission (AFP, 1997a). Given the magnitude and recency of the killings, however, the Rwandan government decided such an approach would be inappropriate to achieve justice and unacceptable to innocent survivors.

The Karamira Case

The arrest and trial of Froduald Karamira highlighted Rwanda's early struggle to seize and prosecute category one suspects.[1] During the 1994 genocide, Karamira, a wealthy businessman and political leader, traveled around Kigali in his Mercedes with an entourage of soldiers, stopping at roadblocks where the corpses of Tutsi and Hutu moderates were piling up. He also made inflammatory broadcasts daily, inciting Hutu to kill their Tutsi neighbors. His fanatical efforts to foment the genocide earned him sixteenth place on the new Rwandan government's list of the top 466 principal presumed commanders, organizers and perpetrators of the genocide (AFP, 1996a).

Ironically, Karamira had been considered a Tutsi. Back in 1990, when a Tutsi refugee army invaded Rwanda from Uganda, Karamira, who then had a Tutsi identification card, was arrested and imprisoned for six months as a rebel sympathizer. He subsequently rejected his Tutsi identification, transformed himself into a Hutu, and became a fanatic to prove his loyalty. In 1993, the opposition party Karamira had founded–the Democratic Republican Movement (DRM)–split. Karamira named his faction MDR-Power and sided with the 'Hutu Power' movement that helped spawn the ideology that advocated genocide. In fact, he is credited with having coined the 'Hutu Power' slogan.

During the 1994 massacres, Karamira flew to New Delhi. Shortly thereafter, the RPF took control of Rwanda and Karamira applied for refugee status in India. Rwandan authorities tracked him down and asked India to extradite him back to Rwanda. In June 1996, Indian immigration authorities called Karamira to their office purportedly to renew his visa. But instead, they put him on a plane to Kigali with a stop in Addis Ababa, Ethiopia.

Once in Addis Ababa, Karamira managed to sneak out of the transit lounge to avoid the final leg of his flight to Kigali. Upon Rwanda's urging, Ethiopian officials captured Karamira, but did not immediately ship him off to Kigali. According to Ethiopian law, a person who enters the country without a visa must be returned to the country of origin–in this case, India. For six weeks Karamira sat in an Ethiopian prison while the press reported that the ICTR and Kigali were making competing claims for his extradition. 'The spokesman of a UN tribunal investigating genocide, Alain Sigg, said the prosecution had formally approached the Rwandan government for talks which may include a possible demand for Karamira to face justice in the tribunal's seat in Arusha in northern Tanzania' (Tadesse, 1996).

Rwanda's Deputy Justice Minister Gerard Gahima expressed anger over what he termed the ICTR's 'interference.' He is quoted as saying, 'We're the ones spending the money and time to get these people, but every time we get them arrested the tribunal appears on the scene to take them. This is unacceptable' (Kaban, 1996). At the time, Rwanda and the ICTR were competing for suspects being held in Cameroon.

Kigali pursued its quest at the highest levels. On 20 June Rwandan President Pasteur Bizimungu made a stopover in Addis Ababa on his return trip from China and Japan to personally ask Ethiopian President Negasso Gidada for Karamira's extradition. Three days earlier, Deputy Justice Minister Gahima had flown there on what Kigali described as 'an urgent mission' to get Karamira for Rwanda.

Finally, on 15 September Karamira, the 'notorious genocide suspect,' arrived in Kigali (BBC, 1996). He became the first alleged genocidaire to be extradited to Rwanda by a foreign country. News correspondent Alan Zarembo (1998) reported that 'Rwanda won the fight for Karamira, a top Rwandan official told me, after [Rwandan authorities] would not guarantee the safety of UN investigators [in Rwanda] if the tribunal did not give up its claim.'

Amnesty International (AI) criticized the ICTR for allegedly not strenuously pursuing its request to the government of Ethiopia for Karamira's surrender, thereby allowing him to go to Kigali were he was sure to be executed. AI, which opposes the death penalty, reasoned that the ICTR should have relied on its statutory primacy over national courts. If Karamira were tried by the Tribunal, his maximum penalty upon conviction would be life in prison. In a press release dated 29 April 1998, the Tribunal responded to AI's criticism by saying that 'the ICTR did not file a request for the surrender of Mr. Karamira with the Ethiopian authorities, let alone fail to "strenuously pursue" it as alleged by Amnesty' (ICTR/INFO-9-2-117).

However, Madeline Morris, a professor of law at Duke University, writes that the Rwandan Minister of Justice met with ICTR Prosecutor Goldstone in Geneva and impressed him with the extensive efforts that Rwanda had expended in gaining custody of Karamira. 'Several hours after the meeting,' Morris writes, 'the ICTR Prosecutor informed the Ethiopian government that he was withdrawing his request for the detention of Karamira until the earlier request of the Rwandan government had been acted upon' (Morris, 1997, p. 365). William A. Schabas (1997), a professor of law at the University of Quebec and an expert on the Rwandan judicial system, wrote that 'the international tribunal eventually backed down in the tug-of-war with Rwandan authorities [over Karamira]. The tribunal recognized that Rwanda needed to judge at least a few of the big fish.'

Now sensitive to charges by human rights organizations that its first trials did not afford defendants proper due process, the Rwandan government announced that Karamira's trial would be in compliance with international conventions, with the right of representation by a lawyer (AFP, 1996a). The government kept its word.

Karamira went on trial in Kigali in mid-January 1997. He pleaded innocent to over a dozen charges, including genocide, crimes against humanity, and murder. Hundreds of citizens elbowed their way into the courtroom to view the short, stocky defendant. Witnesses described the horror that Karamira had inflicted on their lives. One man recited the names of his wife, five children, mother, four sisters, and two nephews, all allegedly murdered at Karamira's urging. A woman claimed Karamira had killed her husband and twenty-six of her neighbors. Another witness, a genocide survivor now missing an eye and an ear, testified that he had observed Karamira order armed thugs to kill a woman at a roadblock in Kigali. Another witness derisively shouted 'Hutu Power' in Karamira's face. The spectators roared!

Paul Kato Atita, a lawyer from Benin in West Africa who was engaged by ASF to defend Karamira, asked the judge for a fifteen-day adjournment. Atita explained that having just arrived in Kigali he needed more time to examine his client's file and take witness statements. The spectators jeered when Karamira told the court that a rejection of his lawyer's request would amount to a denial of his human rights (Megreal 1997). The judge granted the adjournment.

The trial resumed in February. When Karamira took the stand, he showed no remorse. He denied there had been an organized genocide, insisting instead that there had been spontaneous tribal massacres by both Tutsi and Hutu. When the judge confronted him with transcripts of his inciting radio broadcasts, Karamira claimed they had been taken out of context and misedited. He refused to recognize the legitimacy of the court or the new Rwandan government. His defiance angered Tutsi and moderate Hutu around the country who stopped whatever they were doing to listen to Karamira's testimony on their radios. In his final statement, Karamira said 'if my death will make some people happy, then I'm not afraid to die' (Megreal, 1997).

The court pronounced Karamira guilty on 14 February and sentenced him to execution by firing squad. The court also ordered Karamira's property seized so that the equivalent of $3 million could be paid as compensation to survivors of the genocide. Karamira appealed his conviction, claiming that the court had not respected his right to confront witnesses. The appellate court upheld the conviction in September.

On 25 April 1998, policemen led Karamira and three other convicts–two school administrators and a former prosecutor–onto a soccer field in Kigali where they would soon die. The government had refused to honor appeals for a stay of execution by the Pope, the European Union, the United States, and various human rights organizations. All were troubled by the short and inadequate trials. They also worried that the executions might incite renewed conflict.

The police tied each convict to a post, placed black hoods over their heads, and hung bibs bearing rectangular targets on their chests. Over ten-thousand Rwandans gathered to witness the first execution of persons convicted of genocide. Twenty minutes later, four policemen opened fire with their assault rifles on the convicts. A police captain then walked up to the four slumped bodies and fired his pistol twice into each head. Some in the crowd cheered; other simply nodded their heads and walked away. Was this the beginning of reconciliation or revenge?

On the same day, eighteen other persons convicted of genocide were executed in a similar manner in the towns of Gikongoro, Nyamata, Murambi, and Kibungo. By then 346 persons had been tried in Rwandan courts. Over one hundred had been convicted of genocide and sentenced to death. Another hundred were sentenced to life in prison, while an equal number received shorter sentences for their crimes. Only twenty-eight were acquitted.

More Recent Developments

The arrests of persons suspected of being involved in the 1994 massacres and looting continued from 1994 to the time of this writing in 1999. In 1995 and 1996 committees were set up to denounce suspects (*comités de délation*). According to official figures, 125,028 prisoners suspected of genocide and related crimes were being held prisoner in January 1999 (AFP, 1999). Between 1994 and January 1999, 34,000 prisoners had been released. These included sick, aged, and invalid detainees and those against whom there was insufficient evidence. Supreme court public prosecutor Simeon Rwagasore reported that Rwandan courts had tried 864 genocide suspects in 1998 and 3,143 cases were ongoing in January 1999. The courts had handed down over one hundred death sentences since trials began in 1996, but only twenty-two persons had thus far been executed (AFP, 1999). There had been an evolution in the severity of sentencing. Between December 1996 and December 1997, 45 per cent of those accused were given the death penalty, and only 6 per cent were acquitted. In 1998 the proportion of death sentences fell to 16 per cent and acquittals rose to 17 per cent (ICG, 1999).

Rwandan authorities released nearly two thousand prisoners between October 1998 and March 1999. The Rwandan League for the Promotion and Defense of Human Rights (*Ligue Rwandaise pour la Promotion et la Défense des Droits de l'Homme*) set up a project (*Programme de Suivi des Accusés de Génocide mis en liberté* - PSAG) to monitor the situation of the freed genocide suspects in this group. The League's stated aim was to 'contribute to the protection and social reintegration of people who have been the object of judicial pursuit for genocide and who are innocent or presumed innocent.' The following information comes from PSAG's first report, based on investigations carried out between December 1998 and March 1999.[2]

According to PSAG findings, of the 1,988 people released, 1,107 (56%) were freed for lack of evidence, 753 (38%) because they did not have files, fifty-five (2.7%) because they had been acquitted, four (0.2%) because they had served their sentence, nineteen (1%) because they were minors, and fifty (2.5%) because they were elderly. The PSAG team gathered these figures from court prosecutors, presidents of tribunals, and prison directors. The League believes a greater number of genocide suspects would be released if there were more judicial staff to deal with the large prison population. There are far too few judicial personnel given the number of cases to be dealt with.

The report explained that state prosecutors in the southern town of Butare and the central town of Gitarama refused to supply PSAG investigators with names of freed detainees and certain other information about them. The PSAG team found that people released from prison in these two towns were frequently subject to hostile reactions, sometimes even leading to death. Twenty-four freed prisoners were killed in Butare in 1997, and fourteen people belonging to the family of a freed pastor were massacred in Gitarama in 1998.

The PSAG team interviewed 75 of the freed detainees in fifteen communes. The 75 constituted only 4 per cent of the total number freed. Their fifteen communities were distributed through seven of Rwanda's twelve prefectures.

The limited sample was due to a number of factors. The PSAG team found it difficult in towns to locate the homes of many people on their list. Five years after the genocide, many towns contained people from abroad as well as displaced persons from other parts of Rwanda. Consequently, many town dwellers do not know each other, even if they are neighbors. In addition, many freed prisoners had changed their addresses, and their former neighbors were reluctant to reveal their new locations for fear of exposing them to re-arrest. Some freed detainees had been re-arrested. Also, the team simply could not reach some of the more remote settlements where freed persons reportedly resided. But despite the small sample, the findings may reveal some general trends.

PSAG learned that of the 75 people interviewed, 62.6 per cent had been farmers before being imprisoned; 6.6 per cent had been teachers, and 8.8 per cent had been public service workers or NGO employees. With respect to age, 52 per cent were between 20 and 40 years old and 26.6 per cent were 40 to 60. Sixteen or 21.3 per cent said their prison conditions had been relatively good, while 52 or 69.3 per cent claimed they had been subject to beatings, physical torture and abuse. Nine of them were still physically handicapped or had chronic health problems as a result.

PSAG maintains that people who were accused of genocide and later freed face a pitiful life, devoid of basic necessities. Most of their homes had been looted and ransacked. Their families were financially strained, because they had devoted much of their time and resources to supporting imprisoned relatives. Many children of prisoners left school for lack of fees. Most people who were employed before being arrested encounter problems getting their jobs back. Those who were acquitted by the tribunals, however, were able to exercise their right to be rehired and rarely suffered threats.

PSAG reports that almost all interviewees claimed their arrests were linked to their property or their jobs. But, they expressed no desire for revenge against those who had denounced them. They did not plan to start judicial proceedings against such people, as is their legal right, because they said they wanted to live peacefully with everyone, including those who falsely accused them.

The report also enumerates the demands of freed genocide suspects. These include receiving compensation as provided by law, social reintegration, state aid for their children who had been forced to leave school, and state subsidies for those living in dire poverty. Freed detainees who had jobs wanted them back, while torture victims wanted financial help to cover medical costs.

The PSAG team also interviewed genocide survivors. The majority of them said they thought judicial decisions were tainted with corruption, both with regard to genocide trials and the provisional release of genocide suspects. They expressed no confidence in the verdicts handed down. Some survivors opposed the release of minors, the elderly, and chronically sick, because they believed everyone who participated in the genocide should be punished. Most survivors hoped to receive some of the money awarded by court judgments as damages and interest.

Mayors and local officials contacted by PSAG claimed that freed detainees find their property and live peacefully with the local population, who accept them. However, if local residents know that a freed person had played a prominent role in the genocide, they inform authorities, who may re-arrested him. Mayors and local officials also claimed there were successful public campaigns to promote national reconciliation and the reintegration of freed suspects.

Military Justice

The War Council and the Military Court have responsibility for applying the genocide law to acts committed by members of the military. These same bodies also deal with crimes allegedly committed by military personnel against civilians. In his report to the Bar Association of New York, Van Lierop (1997) wrote that 'subsequent to the genocide, the current government has also arrested and charged perhaps over 1,000 of its own soldiers, including officers, for revenge killings and other more common crimes. Under the circumstances, this accountability is an admirable effort to maintain discipline, instill respect for the rule of law, and build a viable system of justice in Rwanda for the first time in the country's history.'

However, in a more recent report, the International Crisis Group (1999) maintains that military cases are not treated with equal severity and far fewer cases have been dealt with than the number of illegal acts recorded. A 1994 UN Human Rights Mission reportedly noted reprisals and indiscriminate massacres carried out by the army in Kibeho, Kanama, and Muramba. Des Forges (1999, 705-735) also lists many purported instances of RPF violations and asserts that very few soldiers have been brought to trial.

The ICTR also has jurisdiction over crimes against humanity, genocide, and related crimes that may have been committed by RPF troops in 1994. However the ICTR appears unlikely to issue any indictments against RPF members. Should it do so, relations between Rwanda and the ICTR, especially its Office of the Prosecutor in Kigali, might break down completely.

Conclusion

Rwanda has been faced simultaneously with a wide array of social, economic, governmental, and judicial challenges. It must integrate millions of mutually distrustful Hutu and Tutsi, including hundreds of thousands of newly arrived Tutsi who were born and raised abroad. The government and military are fully committed to the fight against impunity as an essential condition for national reconciliation and reconstruction. Five years after the genocide, however, many Rwandans and international observers believe that the process is too slow, lacks proper controls, and may be incapable of fulfilling Rwanda's goals of social reconciliation and reintegration.

Nonetheless, Rwanda's attempts at justice, given its deep poverty and devastated infrastructure, represent a unique attempt to fight impunity for genocide and achieve social harmony. Starting as it did from ground zero, the newly created judiciary has achieved some notable results during its first few years. The Rwandan government and the various countries and organizations that are aiding it have made some progress in ensuring the prosecution of many involved in the genocide.

Notes

1. This section is based on a dozen news accounts found in the Nexus-Lexis Library under the search word 'Karamira.'
2. Available at www.hirondelle.org.

6 The Kambanda Case

During 1998 the ICTR made significant progress in the prosecution of persons responsible for the 1994 genocide of Tutsi and moderate Hutu in Rwanda. The case against Rwandan ex-premier Jean Kambanda established essential facts concerning what happened in Rwanda during those fateful 100 days in 1994.[1] Kambanda's extensive admissions of guilt should dispel forever any doubts about the occurrence of a premeditated genocide in Rwanda.

In addition, this case represents a milestone for international humanitarian law. Jean Kambanda is the first person in history to accept responsibility for genocide before an international court. He did so fifty years after the UN adopted the Convention on the Prevention and Punishment of the Crime of Genocide in 1948.

Kambanda's Background

Jean Kambanda, the highest-ranking former political leader in ICTR custody, was born on 10 October 1955 at Mubumbano in the southern Rwandan Prefecture of Butare. He holds the *Diploma d'Ingenieur Commercial*, and in 1994 he had a wife and two children. From May 1989 to April 1994, he worked at the Union des Banques Populaires du Rwanda, rising to the position of bank director. With Swiss backing, the bank promoted economic development in rural areas, where Kambanda first came into contact with what the politicians called the 'rural masses.' His work and influence among the people may have given Kambanda the idea of pursuing a political career when multi-party politics was allowed in Rwanda in June 1991.

Kambanda became one of the first members of the *Mouvement Democratique Republican* (MDR)–the party of former President Gregoire Kayibanda, who had been overthrown in July 1973 by General Juvenal Habyarimana. Kambanda was elected vice president of the MDR in Butare prefecture. During the course of the 1990-92 conflict between the Habyarimana government and the then rebel army of the RPF, the MDR split into two factions, a moderate element in favor of peace negotiations, and an opposing, hard-line 'Hutu Power' group that included Kambanda.

Kambanda claimed that soldiers came to his door on 8 April 1994 while he was in the bath. Fearing for his life, he quickly put on his trousers, jumped out the window, and ran into a banana grove to hide. The soldiers caught up with him, but rather than kill him, they enlisted him to lead the new, radical government (McGreal, 1998). Kambanda claimed he did not want the job, but the soldiers made it clear that he had no choice. Fearing for his family's safety, Kambanda says, he went along.

Shortly after Habyarimana's plane crash, Hutu extremists had slaughtered the previous premier, Agathe Uwilingiyamana, and the ten Belgian United Nations troops protecting her (Prunier, 1997, p. 230). Uwilingiyamana, Rwanda's first female premier, had been opposed to the Hutu Power politicians who planned the genocide. Hence, she was one of the first to be murdered. Kambanda was the obvious choice to succeed her, because he had been the extremist candidate for prime minister the previous year.

Kambanda claims that not he, but Colonel Theoneste Bagosora, was the one behind the planned genocide. However, the 'reluctant' premier played his role well. During the killing rampage, he appeared on television, sporting an army cap and distributing machetes at barricades to Hutu militias, who used them to hack their unarmed victims to death. In one radio address, he announced falsely that the 'war' was over and that it was safe for Tutsi to come out of hiding. Those who did were mercilessly killed.

As the RPF advanced towards Kigali in July 1994, Kambanda and other Hutu leaders of the genocide regime, such as President Theodore Sindikubwabo, fled to Bukavu in Zaire. From there Kambanda fled to Nairobi, Kenya, where President Daniel arap Moi was providing refuge for members of Rwanda's Hutu regime. He and other genocide conspirators feared a Rwandan firing squad more than a Tribunal trial.

As part of a secret plan, which the ICTR labeled 'NAKI' (short for Nairobi-Kigali), Kenyan authorities arrested Kambanda and six other Rwandans on 18 July 1998 at the Tribunal's request. Displaying its new spirit of cooperation, Kenya turned the seven over to the ICTR for trial. The six arrested in addition to Kambanda were: former Minister of Family and Social Welfare Pauline Ntahobali; her son, Arsene Shalom Ntahobali; Army Colonel Gratien Kabiligi; editor-in-chief of *Kangura* and lead genocide propagandist, Hassan Ngeze; Sylvain Nsabimana, the former Prefét of Butare, the site of many anti-Tutsi massacres; and former Commander of the Para-Commando Battalion of the Rwandan Army, Aloys Ntabakuze (ICTR/INFO-9-2).

The arrests meant that the ICTR, after a slow start, then had more high ranking suspects in custody than did its sister institution–The UN International Criminal Tribunal for the Former Yugoslavia–at The Hague. The ICTR was also holding the first women ever indicted by an international criminal tribunal–Pauline Ntahobali.

The Indictment

The prosecutor's office submitted its indictment against Kambanda on 16 October 1997 to Judge Yakov Ostrovsky (Russia), who confirmed it, issued a warrant of arrest against the accused and ordered his continued detention. The indictment contained six counts, namely genocide, conspiracy to commit genocide, direct and public incitement to commit genocide, complicity in genocide, crimes against humanity (murder) punishable under Article 3(a) of the ICTR Statute, and crimes against humanity (extermination) punishable under Article 3(b) of the ICTR Statute. On 1 May 1998, during his initial appearance before Trial Chamber I, consisting of Judges Laity Kama (Senegal), Lennart Aspegren (Sweden), and Navanethem Pillay (South Africa), Kambanda pleaded guilty to all six counts.

Genocide, as defined in the 1948 Convention for the Prevention and Punishment of the Crime of Genocide and in the Statute of the ICTR (Art. 2), is a specific intent crime. Thus, for a crime of genocide to have been committed, it is necessary that one of the acts (e.g., killing, causing serious bodily or mental harm, etc.) listed under Article 2(2) of the ICTR Statute be committed against a specifically targeted 'national, ethnical, racial or religious group' with the intent to destroy it, in whole or in part. A potential defense for many Rwandan genocide suspects is that the 1994 killings were part of an ordinary war or civil upheaval, without any intent to destroy a particular national, ethnical, racial or religious group, in whole or in part. Significantly, however, Kambanda admitted that the extermination of Tutsi was a policy of his government.

Kambanda's Admissions

In his guilty plea Kambanda admitted all the relevant facts alleged in the indictment. In particular, (i) he admitted that there was in Rwanda in 1994 a widespread and systematic attack against the civilian population of Tutsi, with the intent to exterminate them.[2] Mass killings of hundreds of thousands of Tutsi occurred in Rwanda, including women and children, old and young who were pursued and killed at places where they had sought refuge, such as prefectures, commune offices, schools, churches, and stadiums. (ii) Kambanda acknowledged that as prime minister of the interim government of Rwanda from 8 April 1994 to 17 July 1994, he was head of the twenty-member Council of Ministers and exercised de jure authority and control over the members of his government. The government determined and controlled national policy and had the administration and armed forces at its disposal. As prime minister, he also exercised de jure and de facto authority over senior civil servants and senior officers in the military. (iii) Kambanda acknowledged that he participated in meetings of the Council of Ministers, cabinet meetings, and meetings of préféts where the course of massacres were actively followed, but took no action to stop them. Kambanda also acknowledged participation in the dismissal of the préfet of Butare, because the latter had opposed the massacres and the appointment of a new préfet to ensure the spread of massacre of Tutsi in Butare. (iv) Kambanda acknowledged his participation in a high-level security meeting at Gitarama in April 1994 between President T. Sindikubwabo, the Chief of Staff of the Rwandan Armed Forces (FAR), himself, and others, who discussed FAR's support in the fight against the Rwandan Patriotic Front (RPF) and its 'accomplices,' understood to be the Tutsi and moderate Hutu.

In addition, (v) Kambanda acknowledged that he issued the Directive on Civil Defense addressed to the préféts on 25 May 1994 (Directive No. 024-0273, disseminated on 8 June 1994). Kambanda further admitted that this directive encouraged and reinforced the Interahamwe who were committing mass killings of the Tutsi civilian population in the prefectures. Kambanda further acknowledged that by this directive the government assumed responsibility for the actions of the Interahamwe. (vi) Kambanda acknowledged that before 6 April 1994, political parties in concert with the Rwandan Armed Forces organized and began the military training of the youth wings of the MRND and CDR political parties (Interahamwe and Impuzamugambi, respectively) with the intent to use them in the massacres that ensued. Kambanda acknowledged that the government headed by him distributed arms and ammunition to these groups. Additionally, Kambanda confirmed that roadblocks manned by mixed patrols of the Rwandan Armed Forces and the Interahamwe were set up in Kigali and elsewhere as soon as the death of President J.B. Habyarimana was announced on the radio. He also acknowledged the use of the media as part of the plan to mobilize and incite the population to commit massacres of the civilian Tutsi population. That apart,

Kambanda acknowledged the existence of groups within military, militia, and political structures that had planned the elimination of the Tutsi and Hutu political opponents.

In addition, (vii) Kambanda acknowledged that, on or about 21 June 1994, in his capacity as prime minister, he gave clear support to Radio Television *Libre des Mille Collines* (RTLM), with the knowledge that it was a radio station whose broadcasts incited killing, the commission of serious bodily or mental harm to, and persecution of Tutsi and moderate Hutu. On this occasion, speaking on this radio station, Kambanda, as prime minister, encouraged the RTLM to continue to incite the massacres of the Tutsi civilian population, specifically stating that this radio station was 'an indispensable weapon in the fight against the enemy.' (viii) Kambanda acknowledged that following numerous meetings of the Council of Ministers between 8 April 1994 and 17 July 1994, he, as prime minister, instigated, aided, and abetted the préféts, *bourgmestres*, and members of the population to commit massacres and killings of civilians, in particular Tutsi and moderate Hutu.

Furthermore, between 24 April 1994 and 17 July 1994, Kambanda and ministers of his government visited several prefectures, such as Butare, Gitarama (Nyabikenke), Gikongoro, Gisenyi, and Kibuye, to incite and encourage the population to commit these massacres. He also congratulated the people who had committed these killings. (ix) Kambanda acknowledged that on 3 May 1994, he was personally asked to take steps to protect children who had survived the massacre at a hospital, but he did not respond. On the same day, after the meeting, the children were killed. He acknowledged that he failed in his duty to ensure the safety of the children and the population of Rwanda. (x) Kambanda admitted that, in the name of the government, he addressed public meetings and the media at various places in Rwanda directly and publicly inciting the population to commit acts of violence against Tutsi and moderate Hutu.

Furthermore, (xi) Kambanda acknowledged that he ordered the setting up of roadblocks with the knowledge that these roadblocks were used to identify Tutsi for elimination, and that as prime minister he participated in the distribution of arms and ammunition to members of political parties, militias, and the population knowing that these weapons would be used in the perpetration of massacres of civilian Tutsi. (xii) Kambanda acknowledged that he knew or should have known that persons for whom he was responsible were committing crimes of massacre upon Tutsi and that he failed to prevent them or punish the perpetrators. Finally, Kambanda admitted that he was an eye witness to the massacres of Tutsi and also had knowledge of them from cabinet discussions and regular reports of préféts.

After determining Kambanda had entered his guilty plea voluntarily and knowingly, without threats or promises, the Trial Chamber, on 1 May 1998, accepted his plea and found him guilty on all six counts of the indictment.

The Sentence

In determining Kambanda's sentence, the Trial Chamber considered three mitigating factors offered by the defense attorney: 1) Kambanda's guilty plea; 2) the remorse, which the defense attorney claimed was evident from the act of pleading guilty; and 3) Kambanda's past and future cooperation with the Prosecutor's Office. The prosecutor confirmed that Kambanda had extended substantial cooperation and invaluable information to him, and that Kambanda agreed to testify for the prosecution in future trials of other accused.

Just prior to his guilty plea, on 28 April 1998, Kambanda had submitted to Trial Chamber I a document entitled 'Plea Agreement between Jean Kambanda and the Office of the Prosecutor,' signed by himself and his defense counsel, Oliver Michael Inglis from Cameroon. The plea agreement expressly stated that no agreements, understandings or promises had been made between the parties with respect to sentence, which is at the discretion of the Trial Chamber. In the plea agreement, however, the deputy prosecutor disclosed that he had recognized Kambanda's cooperation by promising protective measures for his family to alleviate concerns Kambanda had for their safety.

Kambanda declared in the plea agreement that he had resolved to plead guilty even before his arrest in Kenya and that his prime motivation for pleading guilty was the profound desire to tell the truth, as the truth was the only way to restore national unity and reconciliation in Rwanda. Kambanda considered his confession as a contribution towards the restoration of peace in Rwanda.

However, the Trial Chamber noted that Jean Kambanda had offered no explanation for his voluntary participation in the genocide; nor has he expressed contrition, regret, or sympathy for the victims in Rwanda, even when given the opportunity to do so by the Chamber during the hearing of 3 September 1998.

The defense counsel in his submissions maintained that Jean Kambanda was only a puppet controlled by certain military authorities and that his power was consequently limited. He asked the Tribunal to take that into account as well as the guilty plea, Kambanda's cooperation with the prosecutor, and the role Kambanda could play in the process of Rwandan national reconciliation. He then asked the Tribunal to sentence Kambanda to a term of imprisonment not exceeding two years.

The Trial Chamber explained that a sentence must reflect the predominant standard of proportionality between the gravity of the offense and the degree of responsibility of the offender. 'Just sentences contribute to respect for the law and the maintenance of a just, peaceful and safe society. The crimes for which Kambanda is responsible carry an intrinsic gravity, and their widespread, atrocious and systematic character is particularly shocking to the human conscience.' The judges went on to say that 'Jean Kambanda committed the crimes knowingly and with premeditation; and, moreover, Jean Kambanda, as Prime Minister of Rwanda was entrusted with the duty and authority to protect the population and he abused this trust.'

The justices concluded that the aggravating circumstances surrounding Kambanda's crimes negated the mitigating circumstances. On 4 September 1998, they sentenced him to a single term of life in prison.

Appeal and Recriminations

Within days after the court's decision, Kambanda's defense counsel, Michael Oliver Inglis, filed an appeal against the life sentence (Hirondelle, 1998a). Inglis argued that the sentence was excessive because the judges failed to consider sufficiently his client's guilty plea and willingness to cooperate with the prosecution.

Deputy Prosecutor Bernard Muna acknowledged that he expected Kambanda to be a key witness in the upcoming trials of former military and political officials accused of genocide and other atrocities committed during 1994. Noting that Kambanda was sentenced to the maximum penalty of life imprisonment, Muna explained that 'The Appeal Court will have to clarify Article 101 of the Rules of Procedure, referring to Article 23 of the Statute, that says that the Trial Chamber shall take into account any mitigating circumstances, including substantial cooperation with the Prosecutor' (*Ibid.*). Muna and others wonder whether Kambanda's penalty, under the circumstances, might dissuade other defendants from confessing. Some observers also wonder whether Kambanda will continue to cooperate with investigators after receiving the maximum sentence.

Disappointed with the life sentence and with attorney Inglis, Kambanda demanded a new lawyer of his choice (Hirondelle, 1998b). On 11 September Kambanda sent a bitter, five-page letter to the ICTR Registry accusing attorney Inglis of working against him. Kambanda wrote: 'Without going as far as putting into question my voluntary and conscious decision to tell the truth to the whole of humanity about the drama of the Rwandan people, regardless of the consequences to myself, permit me to cast doubt over certain practices surrounding my trial and the illusion that some people seem to entertain of having found the sacrificial lamb which will erase the responsibilities of others in the extermination of the Rwandan people' (*Ibid.*).

Kambanda suggested that Inglis, who had been a friend of fellow Cameroonian Deputy Prosecutor Bernard Muna for thirty years, had been hastily appointed to him despite his March 1998 request for Belgian attorney Johan Scheers. Kambanda contended that Inglis had negligently permitted his case to be tainted by 'procedural flaws which border on scandalous.' Kambanda also complained that Inglis had failed to secure his sole request in the plea agreement: protection for his family in exile.

On 5 October the registry informed Kambanda that attorney Scheers' past disciplinary problems with the Tribunal made him an unacceptable choice. The Tribunal removed Scheers, who had represented Jean-Paul Akayesu, from the its list of accredited lawyers in 1996 after Scheers had missed the first day of Akayesu's trial because of a financial dispute with the registry. The decision of the ICTR, dated 31 October 1996, states that a financial dispute with the registry cannot be 'an acceptable reason' for being away on the date agreed with the lawyer himself for the opening of the trial. The decision further states that the absence of a lawyer, based on grounds which are neither acceptable nor justifiable, constitutes 'exceptional circumstances' for the withdrawal of his assignment in accordance with Article 19 of the ICTR Directive on the Assignment of Defense Counsel.

In his reply, dated 9 October, Kambanda asked the registry for authorization to receive visits from his lawyer, Johan Scheers, at the ICTY detention center in The Hague, even though Scheers was not his assigned attorney. The ICTR was detaining Kambanda separately at a safe-house in Dodoma in central Tanzania, while it holds other suspects in Arusha. It appears that Kambanda wants to be transferred to The Hague and may not testify for the ICTR prosecution unless his demands for the Belgian lawyer and protection for his family are met.

Conclusion

Observers will wonder why the prosecution did not also charge Kambanda with violations of Article 3 Common to the 1949 Geneva Conventions and Additional Protocol II thereof, which deal with crimes committed during an armed conflict not of an international nature. Kambanda did admit that he, as prime minister, 'exercised de jure and de facto authority over senior civil servants and senior officers in the military.' He also admitted that he issued the Directive on Civil Defense addressed to the préféts on 25 May 1994 and that this directive encouraged and reinforced the Interahamwe who were committing mass killings of the Tutsi civilian population in the prefectures. Kambanda further acknowledged that by this directive the government assumed responsibility for the actions of the Interahamwe. Consequently, by virtue of the humanitarian law principle of command responsibility, Kambanda is culpable for those violations of Article 3 Common to the 1949 Geneva Conventions and Additional Protocol II committed by the military forces and the Interahamwe.

Importantly, in April 1999, a military court in Switzerland found former civilian Rwandan mayor Fulgence Nitonteze guilty of violations of Common Article 3 of the Geneva Conventions, because he had incited genocide at a town meeting and ordered murder and kidnapping in 1994 (AN, 1999c). The Swiss court concluded that the Geneva Conventions can apply to non-military personnel, such as a local administrative head.

ICTR Trial Chamber I's ruling was not as expansive as that of the Swiss court. Nevertheless, Kambanda's extensive confession concerning his government's intentional and well-advertised policy of genocide constitutes the fundamental fact upon which future ICTR prosecutions will rest. His confession also destroys the credibility, if it existed, of revisionist historians, who claim a genocide never took place. Kambanda's confession will affect all ICTR suspects as well as the over 100,000 suspects imprisoned in Rwanda. Those who are guilty of participating in the genocide may well confess, express remorse, and ask for the court's mercy.

Kambanda could also supply additional pages to Rwanda's recent history by answering questions surrounding the mysterious 6 April 1994 downing of the plane carrying Rwandan President Juvenal Habyarimana.

Notes

1. *Prosecutor vs. Jean Kambanda* (1998). Unless otherwise noted, the facts about Kambanda, his admissions and sentencing come from this source.
2. This section on Kambanda's admissions is presented as it appears in *Prosecutor vs. Jean Kambanda* (1998) with only minor stylistic editing.

7 The Akayesu Case

In September 1998, the ICTR completed its first contested case and achieved another milestone by drawing a jurisprudential road map to justice. The case against former Taba *bourgmestre* (mayor) Jean-Paul Akayesu[1] is significant for a series of reasons: it was the first trial before an international tribunal of someone charged with genocide, and it was the first trial in which an international tribunal conceptualized sexual violence (including rape) as an act of genocide. Also, because this was the ICTR's first judgment based on a contested trial, the justices had to face many jurisprudential issues for the first time. Trial Chamber I's lengthy judgment of 2 September 1998 carefully explicates the facts, reasoning and rules it relied upon to reach its conclusions. By so doing, this Judgment will stand as an historic precedent for future tribunals dealing with similar issues.

Akayesu's Background

Jean-Paul Akayesu, a Rwandan national, was born in 1953. He is married, with five children. Prior to becoming *bourgmestre* of Taba commune in the Gitarama prefecture of Rwanda, he was a teacher, then an inspector of schools. Akayesu entered politics in 1991, becoming a founding member of the *Mouvement Démocratique Républicain* (MDR). He served as chairman of the local wing of the MDR in Taba commune. In April 1993, Akayesu, with the support of several key figures and influential groups in the commune, was elected *bourgmestre* of Taba. He held that position until June 1994, when he fled to Zambia.

Arrest and Indictment

Jean-Paul Akayesu was arrested in Zambia on 10 October 1995. On 22 November 1995, the prosecutor of the Tribunal, pursuant to Rule 40 of the Rules, requested the Zambian authorities to keep Akayesu in detention for a period of ninety days while awaiting the completion of the investigation into potential charges against him. On 3 February 1996, Prosecutor Richard Goldstone submitted an indictment against Akayesu, which was subsequently amended on 17 June 1997 to add rape to the charges (see Appendix C). The final indictment contained a total of fifteen counts individually charging Akayesu with genocide, complicity in genocide, direct and public incitement to commit genocide, extermination, murder, torture, cruel treatment, rape, other inhumane acts and outrages upon personal dignity, crimes against humanity, and violations of Article 3 Common to the 1949 Geneva Conventions and Additional Protocol II thereof. Judge William H. Sekule confirmed the indictment and issued an arrest warrant, accompanied by an order for continued detention, on 16 February 1996. Akayesu was transferred to the ICTR detention facilities in Arusha on 26 May 1996. He pleaded not guilty to all counts in the indictment.

Akayesu was originally defended by Belgian lawyer Johan Scheers. However, Akayesu replaced Scheers on 31 October 1996 with American lawyer Michael Karnavas. Less than a month later, on 22 November 1996, Akayesu rejected Karnavas as well, claiming in a letter to the ICTR that the American lawyer had threatened him by leading him to understand that if he did not accept Karnavas as his defense lawyer, he would be found guilty.

Karnavas (1997, p. 59) denies the charge and offers a different version of events. He maintains that Belgian commercial attorney, Luc de Temmerman, a person closely associated with Mrs. Habyarimana (the former Rwandan president's wife) and her clan, cautioned him that he, Karnevas, was not representing Akayesu, but 'the Hutu nation' and 'the cause.' Karnavas alleges that Temmerman claimed that a genocide had not occurred, that it was simply Tutsi propaganda. According to Karnavas, when he refused to go along with Temmerman's strategy and beliefs, Temmerman accused him of being an agent of the new Rwandan government and a Tutsi spy, who was sabotaging Akayesu's case and 'the cause.' Two weeks later Akayesu fired Karnavas, claiming (according to Karnavas) that the American had 'brainwashed, intimidated, and manipulated' him.

Seven weeks before his trial began Akayesu chose attorneys Nicolas Tiangaye of the Central African Republic and Patrice Monthé of Cameroon from a list of potential defense lawyers prepared by the ICTR Registry, which was also responsible for their compensation. At the opening of the trial on 9 January 1997 Akayesu tried to reject his new lawyers, claiming one of them had been 'bought' by the Tribunal.

Are the Tutsi a Protected Group?

Before determining whether Akayesu was guilty of acts of genocide, Trial Chamber I, consisting of Judges Laity Kama (Senegal), Lennart Aspegren (Sweden), and Navanethem Pillay (South Africa) had to determine whether genocide as defined in Article 2 of the ICTR Statute, which replicates the Genocide Convention, had occurred in Rwanda. According to ICTR Statute Article 2(2),

> Genocide means any of the following acts committed with intent to destroy, in whole or in part, a national, ethnical, racial or religious group as such:
> a) Killing members of the group;
> b) Causing serious bodily or mental harm to members of the group;
> c) Deliberately inflicting on the group conditions of life calculated to bring about its physical destruction in whole or in part;
> d) Imposing measures intended to prevent births within the group;
> e) Forcibly transferring children of the group to another group.

Members of the chamber reasoned that since the special intent to commit genocide lies in the intent to destroy, in whole or in part, a national, ethnical, racial or social group, it was necessary to determine the meaning of these social categories. Because neither the Genocide Convention nor the ICTR Statute had defined them, the task fell upon the justices themselves. Based on their reading of the *travaux préparatoires* (preparatory work) of the Genocide Convention, the justices concluded that the drafters perceived the crime of genocide as targeting only stable, permanent groups, whose membership is determined by birth. The drafters excluded more mobile groups, such as political and economic groups, that one joins voluntarily. The justices then proceeded to define each of the social categories listed in the ICTR Statute:

> Based on the Nottebohm decision rendered by the International Court of Justice, the Chamber holds that a national group is defined as a collection of people who are perceived to share a legal bond based on common citizenship, coupled with reciprocity of rights and duties.
> An ethnic group is generally defined as a group whose members share a common language or culture.
> The conventional definition of racial group is based on the hereditary physical traits often identified with a geographical region, irrespective of linguistic, cultural, national or religious factors.
> The religious group is one whose members share the same religion, denomination or mode of worship.

Significantly, the Tutsi-Hutu distinction in Rwanda does not fit well into any of the above categories. The Tutsi belong to the same religious groups and national group as do the Hutu. The Tutsi and Hutu share a common language and culture. And any hereditary physical traits formerly distinguishing Hutu from Tutsi have become largely obliterated through generations of intermarriage and a classification scheme based on cattle ownership. Consequently, had the ICTR justices stopped here, they would have been forced to conclude that genocide, as legally defined in the Convention and Statute, had not occurred in Rwanda!

Fortunately, the justices did not stop here. They next asked 'whether it would be impossible to punish the physical destruction of a group as such under the Genocide Convention, if the said group, although stable and membership is by birth, does not meet the definition of any one of the four groups expressly protected by the Genocide Convention [and Article 2 of the ICTR Statute].' They concluded that the answer is 'no,' because it is 'important to respect the intention of the drafters of the Genocide Convention, which according to the *travaux préparatoires,* was patently to ensure the protection of any stable and permanent group.'

Next, the chamber asked whether the Tutsi constituted a stable and permanent group for purposes of the Genocide Convention. To answer this question, the chamber considered evidence provided by eye-witness and expert testimony during the trial. The justices noted that the Tutsi constituted a group referred to as 'ethnic' in official Rwandan classifications. Identity cards prior to 1994 included a reference to '*ubwoko*' in Kinyarwanda or '*ethnie*' (ethnic group) in French, which referred to the designations Hutu, Tutsi, and Twa. The chamber observed that all the Rwandan witnesses who appeared before it invariably answered without hesitation the prosecutor's questions regarding their ethnic identity.

Earlier in their judgment, the justices noted that witnesses testified that, 'Even pregnant women, including those of Hutu origin, were killed on the grounds that the foetuses in their wombs were fathered by Tutsi men, for in a patrilineal society like Rwanda, the child belongs to the father's group of origin.' Witness PP testified that Akayesu had made a public statement to the effect that 'if a Hutu woman were impregnated by a Tutsi man, the Hutu woman had to be found in order for the pregnancy to be aborted.' Given these and related facts, the chamber found that at the time of the alleged events, 'the Tutsi did indeed constitute a stable and permanent group and were identified as such by all.' Consequently, they were protected by the Genocide Convention and Article 2 of the ICTR Statute.

The Akayesu Case 99

Here, the chamber made two critical determinations that will greatly influence future cases involving the crime of genocide. By adding 'stable and permanent group, whose membership is largely determined by birth,' to the four existing categories (i.e., national, ethnical, racial, and religious group) of the Genocide Convention, Trial Chamber I significantly expanded the kinds of populations that will be protected by that Convention. The chamber also expanded upon the categories of protected peoples by refusing to confine itself to an objective, universalistic definition of ethnic group. Instead, it relied on the subjective perceptions of the Rwandan people, themselves. Consequently, it established as a precedent the idea that a court may regard any stable and permanent group, whose membership is largely determined by birth, as an ethnic group for purposes of the Genocide Convention as long as the people of the society in question perceive that group to be stable, involuntary in membership, and different from others according to local, subjective criteria.

Determining Intent

As explained above, specific intent is a constitutive element of the crime of genocide. Intent is a mental factor that is difficult to determine with precision in the absence of a sincere confession or public admission by the accused. The chamber provided another jurisprudential roadway by maintaining that, in the absence of a confession, the accused's intent can be inferred from a number of presumptions of fact. The chamber reasoned that 'it is possible to deduce the genocidal intent inherent in a particular act charged from the general context of the perpetration of other culpable acts systematically directed against that same group, whether these acts were committed by the same offender or by others.' Specific factors that the chamber believed could enable it to infer the genocidal intent of a particular act included the scale of atrocities committed, their general nature, and the deliberate and systematic targeting of people because of their membership in a particular group, while excluding members of other groups.

Here, the chamber offers a method for determining an individual's constructive genocidal intent. This method involves placing an accused's particular act(s) against a victim within the broad context of prevalent and culpable acts directed at other persons because they are members of the victim's group, even if these acts were perpetrated by persons other than the accused.

Sexual Violence and Rape as Crimes against Humanity and Genocide

The indictment against Akayesu was submitted on 13 February 1996 by Prosecutor Richard Goldstone and was confirmed on 16 February 1996. Originally, it did not contain specific charges of sexual crimes. However, prosecutors amended the indictment during the trial, in June 1997, and resubmitted it, under the signature of the new Prosecutor, Louise Arbour, with the addition of three counts (13 to 15) and three paragraphs (10A, 12A, and 12B). In introducing the amended indictment, prosecutors stated that the testimony of Witness H motivated them to renew their investigation of sexual violence in connection with events which took place in Taba at the bureau communal. Prosecutors explained that evidence previously available was insufficient to link Akayesu to acts of sexual violence. They reasoned that the lack of evidence might be attributed to the shame that victims of sexual violence feel and an insensitivity in the investigation of sexual violence.

In paragraph 10A, the prosecutor proposes a definition of sexual violence intended to clarify the allegations set forth in paragraphs 12A and 12B. These three paragraphs are reproduced below:

> 10A. In this indictment, acts of sexual violence include forcible sexual penetration of the vagina, anus or oral cavity by a penis and/or of the vagina or anus by some other object, and sexual abuse, such as forced nudity.

> 12A. Between April 7 and the end of June 1994, hundreds of civilians (hereinafter 'displaced civilians') sought refuge at the bureau communal. The majority of these displaced civilians were Tutsi. While seeking refuge at the bureau communal, female displaced civilians were regularly taken by armed local militia and/or communal police and subjected to sexual violence, and/or beaten on or near the bureau communal premises. Displaced civilians were also murdered frequently on or near the bureau communal premises. Many women were forced to endure multiple acts of sexual violence which were at times committed by more than one assailant. These acts of sexual violence were generally accompanied by explicit threats of death or bodily harm. The female displaced civilians lived in constant fear and their physical and psychological health deteriorated as a result of the sexual violence and beatings and killings.

> 12B. Jean Paul AKAYESU knew that the acts of sexual violence, beatings and murders were being committed and was at times present during their commission. Jean Paul AKAYESU facilitated the commission of the sexual violence, beatings and murders by allowing the sexual violence and beatings and murders to occur on or near the bureau communal premises. By virtue of his

presence during the commission of the sexual violence, beatings and murders and by failing to prevent the sexual violence, beatings and murders, Jean Paul AKAYESU encouraged these activities.

Count 13 of the indictment charged Akayesu with rape as a crime against humanity, punishable under ICTR Statute Article 3(g) (which specifically names rape as a crime against humanity). In addressing this charge, the chamber noted that there is no commonly accepted definition of the term 'rape' in international law. It chose to regard rape as a form of aggression and looked to the Convention against Torture and Other Cruel, Inhuman and Degrading Treatment or Punishment for guidance in its formulation of a definition. The chamber observed that that Convention does not catalog specific acts in its definition of torture, but rather focuses on the conceptual framework of state-sanctioned violence. The justices reasoned that rape, like torture, is used for such purposes as 'intimidation, degradation, humiliation, discrimination, punishment, control or destruction of a person.' They further stated that 'like torture, rape is a violation of personal dignity, and rape...constitutes torture when...inflicted by or at the instigation of or with the consent or acquiescence of a public official or other person acting in an official capacity.'

The chamber also reasoned that acts constituting crimes against humanity have four essential elements:

(i) the act must be inhumane in nature and character, causing great suffering, or serious injury to body or to mental or physical health;
(ii) the act must be committed as part of a widespread or systematic attack;
(iii) the act must be committed against members of the civilian population;
(iv) the act must be committed on one or more discriminatory grounds, namely, national, political, ethnic, racial or religious grounds.

With these elements in mind, the chamber defined rape and sexual violence for purposes of Crimes against Humanity as:

a physical invasion of a sexual nature, committed on a person under circumstances which are coercive. Sexual violence which includes rape, is considered to be any act of a sexual nature which is committed on a person under circumstances which are coercive. This act must be committed: (a) as part of a widespread or systematic attack; (b) on a civilian population; (c) on certained catalogued discriminatory grounds, namely: national, ethnic, political, racial, or religious grounds.

Further on in the judgment, the chamber stated that 'sexual violence is not limited to physical invasion of the human body and may include acts which do not involve penetration or even physical contact.' The chamber noted as an example of sexual violence the incident described by Witness KK in which Akayesu ordered the Interahamwe to undress a student and force her to do gymnastics naked before a crowd in the public courtyard of the bureau communal. Hence, by not confining sexual violence to cases of bodily penetration, the chamber agreed with the definition of sexual violence offered by the Prosecutor in paragraph 10A of the indictment (quoted above).

The chamber found that there was sufficient credible evidence to establish beyond a reasonable doubt that Tutsi girls and women were subjected to sexual violence, beaten, and killed on or near the bureau communal premises, as well as elsewhere in the commune of Taba in 1994. The chamber also found beyond a reasonable doubt that Akayesu knew or had reason to know that sexual violence was being inflicted on those women who were kept at the bureau communal and on those who were taken from there. The chamber found no evidence that the accused took any measures to prevent acts of sexual violence or to punish the perpetrators. To the contrary, there was evidence that Akayesu ordered, instigated, aided, and abetted sexual violence. Consequently, the chamber found Akayesu guilty of rape as a crime against humanity.

Count 1 of the indictment charged Akayesu with the crime of genocide, punishable under Article 2(3)(a) of the Statute, which simply lists 'genocide' as one of the acts of genocide. Count 1 made no specific reference to sexual violence or rape. However, among the definitions of genocide offered by Article 2(2) is 'causing serious bodily or mental harm to members of a group.'

The Tribunal *sua sponte* (on its own motion) chose to consider sexual violence in connection with Count 1 and the allegations made in paragraphs 12(A) and 12(B) of the indictment (quoted above). The three justices reasoned that the acts of rape and sexual violence contained in the indictment constituted genocide in the same way as any other act listed under 'Genocide' Article 2(2) of the ICTR Statute as long as they were committed with the specific intent to destroy, in whole or in part, a particular group–the Tutsi. Rape and sexual violence certainly constitute inflictions of 'serious bodily and mental harm' on victims. In light of all the evidence before it, the chamber was satisfied that the acts of rape and sexual violence described by witnesses were committed solely against Tutsi women, many of whom were subjected to the worst public humiliation, mutilated, and raped several times, often in public, in the Bureau Communal premises or in other public places, and often by more than one assailant. These rapes, the chamber concluded, resulted in physical and psychological destruction of Tutsi women, their families, and their communities. Sexual violence was an integral part of the process of destruction, specifically targeting Tutsi women and specifically contributing to their destruction and to the destruction of the Tutsi group as a whole.

The Tribunal found that Akayesu had aided and abetted the acts of sexual violence by allowing them to take place in his presence on or near the premises of the bureau communal and by verbally encouraging the commission of these acts. By virtue of his authority, his overt encouragement sent a clear signal of official tolerance for sexual violence, without which these acts would not have taken place. Consequently, the chamber concluded that the acts alleged in paragraphs 12A and 12B of the indictment and subsequently proven at trial constitute the crime of genocide for which it found Akayesu individually criminally responsible.

Witnesses and Testimony

During the seventeen-month-long trial, punctuated by defense-requested adjournments, the justices heard forty-two witnesses (including five expert witnesses). Many of those testifying were eye-witnesses and victims who told gruesome stories of their ordeals. The proceedings generated more than 4000 pages of transcripts and 125 evidentiary documents. The final judgment runs over two hundred pages.

The first person to testify for the prosecution was a 35-year old Tutsi woman, known as Witness JJ to protect her identity.[2] She explained how within days after President Habyarimana's plane crashed, Hutu killed her husband, tore down her family's home, then slaughtered and ate her cows. She fled, with her twenty-month-old son on her back, to the farm of a Hutu neighbor, but he was too scared to hide her, so she and the baby spent the night in a field of coffee plants. The next morning her Hutu neighbor brought her food and advised her to go to the Taba municipal office of mayor Jean-Paul Akayesu, because Tutsi were seeking refuge there.

When she arrived at the municipal compound, about sixty Tutsi, mostly women and children, were already there. She saw Akayesu standing next to two policemen armed with pistols. Soon, she said, Hutu thugs began beating her, her child, and many of the other Tutsi refugees. Witness JJ fled to a nearby banana plantation, but a policeman found her there and beat her with the butt of his pistol. The next morning Witness JJ and about ten other Tutsi women went to Akayesu and asked him to shoot them, because they could no longer endure the brutal beatings, saying,. 'He told us there were no more bullets, and even if there were, they would not waste them on us. He had the police chase us away.'

Witness JJ and the other women went back to the banana plantation. Shortly thereafter soldiers came and began raping the women. The next day some soldiers took Witness JJ and some other women to the communal office, known as the 'cultural center,' where drunken soldiers were raping screaming girls. Three of them also raped Witness JJ. The next day she was raped twice more. The rapes were especially humiliating because many took place in public, before children. She testified that Akayesu told the rapist, 'Don't tell me that you won't have tasted a Tutsi woman. Take advantage of it, because they'll be killed tomorrow.' 'He spoke as though he were encouraging players,' she said.

Desperate and weak, she took her child and limped off to a corn field. Later, she accepted the offer of a Hutu couple who said they would care for her baby while she was on the run. They had a cow and said they would give the child milk. Instead, Witness JJ testified, they killed the baby and let their dogs eat his body. Somehow, she escaped with her life. She met with ICTR prosecutors in June 1997.

According to Witness JJ 'Akayesu did not kill with his own hands, but with his orders.' She said that Akayesu had declared all Tutsis as enemy and had asked the Hutu to get rid of them. He made the call at a public meeting in Taba on 19 April 1994, following a 'security' meeting of mayors and members of the interim government in Murambi the day before. Witness JJ claimed Akayesu specifically told people 'if you knew what the Tutsis were doing. I have just found out at the security meeting. I have no more pity for them, especially the intellectuals. I will give them to you.'

In cross-examination, the defense asked Witness JJ how Akayesu was to blame for her ordeal. 'Did he have the means to prevent the rapes?' She responded that Akayesu was an authority. He could have protected the women and children, but he did nothing for them. 'When I went to see him for help, he had the police get me away.'

Other witnesses would also testify to Akayesu's change in attitude following the security meeting held twelve days after the start of the genocide.

Witness C, a male Hutu peasant farmer, was the second witness. He told the court that Akayesu had thugs beat him because he refused to tell them the location of a Tutsi woman he was hiding. Witness C took off his shirt in court to reveal the scars he still bore from the torture.

Witness N, a Rwandan women in her fifties, was the third witness for the prosecution. She testified that Akayesu spoke at two rallies where he encouraged Hutu to eliminate Tutsi. She claimed he said, 'When you kill mice you don't spare the babies.'

The ninth witness told how Akayesu had accused Tutsi of 'subversive machinations.' Akayesu allegedly said, 'The Tutsis have been holding meetings and plan to exterminate the Hutu intellectuals so that they can dominate the peasants,' before urging the Hutu population to join militias to wipe out the Tutsi, the 'allies of the *Inkotanyi*' (RPF).

On 16 and 17 January, the court heard testimony from three expatriate witnesses who were in Rwanda during April 1994. Through the testimony of these witnesses, the prosecution wanted to show that the events from April to July 1994 were carried out systematically and were directed against a particular ethnic group, thereby amounting to genocide. The three expatriate witnesses were Dr. Rony Zacharia of *Medecins sans Frontieres*, British cameraman Simon Cox, and British journalist and former UNICEF employee Lindsey Hilsum.

Hilsum, one of only two foreign correspondents in Kigali when the 1994 massacres began, was called to the witness box to describe what he saw. Hilsum (1997) described hearing the rocket attack that brought down the president's plane. He then began receiving desperate phone calls from Tutsi friends who feared being killed. On the third day he ventured out on to the streets and saw menacing bands of armed men (Interahamwe) at roadblocks. He saw the corpses of five women who had been hacked to death. At the hospital he saw blood running in the gutters and stumbled over wounded bodies. She saw a woman with a baby in her arms, its leg partially severed, wandering hopelessly, looking for a doctor.

On 29 and 30 January, professor of linguistics Mathias Ruzindana explained to the court the origin and significance of the Kinyarwanda terms *Inyenzi* and *Inkotanyi*, frequently used by witnesses. He explained that *Inyenzi* (cockroaches) was first applied to the Tutsi resistance fighters at the time of anti-government attacks in 1963. It described their tactics of acting at night and disappearing with the first light. The term eventually came to have pejorative connotations, and by 1994 was used to denote Tutsi in general, the presumed accomplices of the RPF. The RPF gave the name *Inkotanye* (fighter) to their own soldiers. Dr. Ruzindana also explained how the oral tradition of Rwandese culture was responsible for the apparent unreliability of witness testimony in court. For instance, in Rwanda the expression 'I saw' can also mean 'I heard' or 'I know.'

Dr. Alison Des Forges, an American human rights activist and historian, testified on 11 and 12 February as an expert witness on the history of Rwanda. She told the court that thirty years of Belgian colonization had institutionalized in Rwanda the system of ethnic identity cards distinguishing Hutu, Tutsi, and Twa. She maintained that the Belgian administration had contributed considerably to the origins of the genocide by stressing ethnic distinctions and Tutsi superiority.

The judges suspended the trial on 20 May, and on 17 June they approved the prosecution's motion to add three new charges of sexual violence to the indictment.

On 22 October the trial resumed with the testimony of four women who told the court that they had been the victims of sexual violence committed in Taba in 1994. Three of them said that they had been subjected to group rapes by the Interahamwe militia in and around the communal office of Taba, in view of the accused. They testified that between April and May 1994, Tutsi women were raped singly or in groups by multiple assailants who later killed them.

The first defense witnesses were heard on 17 November 1997. The initial three witnesses were natives of Taba imprisoned in Rwanda for their alleged participation in the genocide. The Rwandan authorities facilitated their appearance by handing them over temporarily to the custody of the ICTR. They testified that Akayesu, the former mayor of Taba, had given in to pressure from the Interahamwe militia two weeks after the beginning of the genocide. The accused had initially tried to prevent the Interahamwe from invading his commune, the witnesses said, and he had supported the people, who had killed two militia members. The defense decided not to call a fourth witness, saying that the testimony might damage the accused.

By 9 February, seven out of twelve defense witnesses had refused to appear in court for fear of 'reprisals.' On 10 February another Rwandan witness testified that Akayesu had been under the rule of the Interahamwe. Like the others, this witness supported the defense strategy of portraying Akayesu as a mayor who used his limited authority to do everything possible to protect the population before he, himself, fell hostage to the Interahamwe.

On 10 February, Joseph Matata, the Rwandan director of the Center for the Struggle against Impunity and Injustice, told the court that those indicted by the Rwandan courts and by the ICTR are accused on the basis of orchestrated testimony from so called 'denunciation syndicates' active in Rwanda.

On 13 February, the judges denied the defense's request to call former Prime Minister Jean Kambanda and one of his former ministers to the stand. Both were being detained by the ICTR and had been charged with genocide and crimes against humanity. The judges reasoned that the defenses of the two detainees could be jeopardized if they were required to testify in this case.

On 19 November, at the request of the defense, the Tribunal subpoenaed Canadian General Romeo Dallaire, the former commander of the United Nations Assistance Mission to Rwanda (UNAMIR) between 21 October 1993 and 19 August 1994. The Secretary General of the United Nations, Kofi Annan, who had been responsible for UN peacekeeping operations in 1994, granted the general partial immunity to testify about matters not related to confidential UN communications and documents. Dallaire's communication with UN headquarters, specifically the famous fax from Dallaire to Annan in January 1994, could not be discussed.

Dallaire had already gone public, claiming that if he had been given more troops and a proper mandate, UNAMIR could have saved thousands of Rwandans in 1994. The defense's strategy was to show the judges that if UNAMIR troops had been unable to stop the killing, how could anyone expect Akayesu, a single man, to stop it.

Dressed in his military uniform, General Dallaire entered the courtroom on 25 February 1998. Judge Kama explained that Dallaire was testifying not as a witness for the defense, but as an expert witness requested by the defense. Dallaire told the court that if UNAMIR had been given more troops and was authorized to operate under Chapter VII of the UN Charter (that is, authorized to use military force), it could have intervened during the first few weeks of April and saved whole areas of Rwanda from the massacres. Instead of increasing his 2,500 man force, Belgium pulled out its contingent and the UN Security Council downsized UNAMIR to 450 troops. 'We didn't have the resources to defend ourselves reasonably, let alone to help the people who were coming to us.'

During his five-and-one-half hour testimony, Dallaire spread the blame widely. 'The UN is not a sovereign country. The UN is us, all of us. And if the UN didn't intervene, this means that by extension, we are all responsible for the genocide.' Dallaire paused, took a tissue from his pocket, and wiped tears from his eyes.

On 26 February, the court rejected a defense request to call five additional witnesses. President Kama stated that 'a trial is started in order to be concluded.'

Akayesu testified in his own defense on 12 March. He portrayed himself as a helpless, low-level official who had no control over events in Taba commune. He told the Court that the Interahamwe was responsible for the killings. Akayesu claimed he had asked the Prefét of Gitarama for gendarmes to maintain law and order, but received no support. He said that when he tried to save some Tutsi, he was accused of supporting the RPF and his life was threatened (ICTR/INFO-9-2-110).

Closing Arguments

On 19 March 1998, the prosecution began its closing arguments. Prosecutor Pierre Prosper of the United States said Akayesu, being a government official, 'had the duty to protect the population, and the people looked up to him, but he betrayed them.' The prosecutor acknowledged that prior to a key meeting on 18 April 1994 in Gitarama, Akayesu did oppose the Interahamwe, who had begun killing Tutsi and moderate Hutu. 'However, after the meeting he transformed from protector of the people to a predator, telling the [Hutu] people to forget their political differences and unite to fight the Tutsi.'

Prosper went on to cite several incidents in which Akayesu was in a position to stop the massacres and rapes of women. Instead, however, Akayesu ordered or, at the least, aided and abetted the killings and rapes. Finally, Prosper noted that some people argued that *bourgmestre* Akayesu was only a 'small fish.' 'But for the people of Taba,' the prosecutor stressed, 'he was a barracuda. He was in charge of their security. He had the power to arrest and the power to release. He was a parent figure, who became an assassin' (ICTR/INFO-9-8-008).

Defence attorney Nicolas Tiangaye of the Central African Republic began his closing argument on 26 March 1998. He complained that the indictment had been amended in response to public pressure [from Human Rights Watch and women's rights groups] concerning the prosecution of sexual violence. Later the chamber would note in its judgment that non-governmental organizations had expressed interest in this issue. And Judge Navanethem Pillay of South Africa, Trial Chamber I's only female judge, reportedly told a reporter: 'From time immemorial, rape has been regarded as spoils of war. Now it will be considered a war crime. We want to send out a strong signal that rape is no longer a trophy of war' (Berkeley, 1998).

Attorney Tiangaye continued to characterize Akayesu as a mayor who tried to help his people. He did not change for the worse after the meeting on 18 April in Gitarama, Tiangaye argued, but he did lose de facto control over Taba commune. The real power in Taba and the one responsible for the crimes there was an Interahamwe leader named Silas Kubwimana, Tiangaye insisted. Attorney Tiangaye also challenged the prosecutor's right to speak in the name of the international community, when that same community had not acted to stop the genocide. Tiangaye cited General Dallaire who maintained that if the UN had provided UNAMIR with sufficient troops and changed its mandate, thousands of lives could have been saved (ICTR/INFO-9-2-114). The attorney implied that the same UN that failed Rwanda then was seeking scapegoats for its Tribunal now.

The Verdict

The chamber largely agreed with the prosecution. The judges unanimously found Akayesu guilty of: genocide (Count 1), crime against humanity (extermination) (Count 3), direct and public incitement to commit genocide (Count 4), crime against humanity (murder) (Counts 5, 7 & 9), crime against humanity (torture) (Count 11), crime against humanity (rape) (Count 13), crime against humanity (other inhumane acts) (Count 14). The chamber found him not guilty of: complicity in genocide (Count 2), violations of Article 3 common to the Geneva Conventions (murder) (Counts 6, 8, 10) and (cruel treatment) (Count 12), and violations of Article 3 common to the Geneva Conventions and of Article 4(2)(e) of Additional Protocol II (outrage upon personal dignity, in particular rape, degrading and humiliating treatment, and indecent assault) (Count 15).

Some Final Observations

Who was Akayesu? Correspondent Berkeley (1998) may have answered this question best:

> Jean-Paul Akayesu was neither a psychopath nor a simpleton. He was not a top figure like the former defense minister, Theoneste Bagasora, Rwanda's Himmler, who is now in custody in Arusha, nor a lowly, illiterate, machete-wielding peasant. He was instead, the link between the two: an archetype of the indispensable middle management of the genocide. He personified a rigidly hierarchical society and a culture of obedience, without which killing on such a scale would not have been possible.

Despite the lowly political stature of the defendant, this case has immense factual and jurisprudential importance. This chapter addresses only a limited number of many important issues. With its decision in *Akayesu*, the Trial Chamber expanded the Genocide Convention and Tribunal Statute and introduced a subjective standard for determining what groups in a particular society are protected by the Genocide Convention. Arguably, by definition, there would have been no genocide in Rwanda had the chamber not done this. In addition, the chamber explicated a method for determining an individual's constructive genocidal intent. It also offered definitions of rape and sexual violence for purposes of humanitarian law.

Given Mayor Akayesu's de jure and de facto authority and given the fact that Akayesu, dressed in a military jacket and carrying a military weapon, had accompanied the Interahamwe on some of its criminal missions against civilians, some observers will criticize the chamber for not finding Akayesu guilty of Counts 12 and 15 (violations of Article 3 Common to the 1949 Geneva Conventions and Additional Protocol II). The prosecution has already appealed the not guilty verdicts on these counts. Consequently, the Appeals Chamber in The Hague will have the final word on these issues.

This case has generated some major contributions to humanitarian law; it will also generate voluminous commentary.

Notes

1. *Prosecutor vs. Jean-Paul Akayesu.* (1998) Case No. ICTR 96-4-T, Judgment, 2 Sept. Unless otherwise noted, the information in this chapter comes from this case.
2. Swiss-based Fondation Hirondelle, an independent press agency, covered the proceedings of Akayesu's trial. Its account is found at www.hirondelle.org. In addition to the Hirondelle report, this section dealing with witness testimony is based on: Blanchfield (1998b), AFP (1997c), AFP (1997d), Thompson (1998), Santoro (1998), Gourevitch (1998a), and *Ubutabera* (1998).

8 Conclusion

The 1994 Rwandan genocide represents one of the most tragic events of recent decades. Today, the international community admits that it could have done more to prevent or stop the massacres. Given the difficulties the new Rwanda faces in extraditing the planners and organizers of the genocide from other countries and in trying to judge the guilt or innocence of over 100,000 persons held in prisons under substandard conditions, the ICTR becomes an important institution for ending the culture of impunity.

The establishment of the International Tribunal in 1994 reflected the international community's belief that the prosecution of the perpetrators of genocide and other serious crimes will prevent their repetition and convince Rwandans that justice will prevail. The success of the ICTR is essential for Rwanda's national reconciliation and the prevention of future attempts at genocide.

The United States, Canada, Japan, and the European Union have cooperated closely with the Tribunal by voluntary contributions to a special UN Trust Fund, through assessed contributions, and by seconding experienced legal personnel. African countries have become more cooperative in terms of surrendering indicted persons to the ICTR. The international community must not fail in its commitment to the ICTR as it failed in making concerted efforts in preventing the carnage of 1994.

The ICTR and its predecessor, the ICTY, are also important for the development of international humanitarian law. These two tribunals represent the first attempts by the international community to create international judicial organs to enforce the Geneva Conventions, the Genocide Convention, and laws proscribing crimes against humanity. The Rwandan Tribunal is unique in that it is the first international court to apply crimes against humanity to a non-international conflict and to enforce Article 3 Common and Protocol II of the Geneva Conventions. The extension of its territorial jurisdiction to countries not party to the Rwandan conflict represents another new development in international law.

The exact impact that the ICTR will have on the application of international humanitarian law and the legal prerogatives of the Security Council acting under Chapter VII of the UN Charter will be determined by actual political and judicial experience and the reactions of states. The ICTR's success depends upon international cooperation in apprehending and transferring suspects, in permitting on-site visits and interviews with witnesses, and in securing evidentiary documents.

In 1998 the ICTR set several monumental precedents for international humanitarian law. On 1 May 1998, the Tribunal recorded the first guilty plea on a count of genocide. Jean Kambanda, prime minister of the interim government established in Rwanda after the 1994 air crash in which President Habyarimana was killed, pleaded guilty to all the counts in the indictment against him, including those of genocide, direct and public incitement to commit genocide, complicity in genocide, and crimes against humanity. In pleading guilty, Kambanda not only confirmed that genocide occurred in Rwanda in 1994, but also admitted that it was planned and organized at the highest levels of government.

Kambanda's extensive confession concerning his government's intentional and well-advertised policy of genocide constitutes the fundamental fact upon which future ICTR prosecutions will rest. His confession destroys the credibility of revisionist historians, who claim a genocide never took place. Kambanda's admissions will affect all ICTR suspects as well as the over 100,000 suspects imprisoned in Rwanda. Those who are guilty of participating in the genocide may well confess, express remorse, and ask for the court's mercy.

The ICTR's 2 September 1998 decision in the case of former Taba *bourgmestre* Jean-Paul Akayesu is significant for a series of reasons: it was the first trial before an international tribunal of someone charged with genocide, and it was the first trial in which an international tribunal conceptualized sexual violence as an act of genocide. Also, because this was the ICTR's first judgment based on a contested trial, the justices dealt with some important jurisprudential issues for the first time.

With its decision in *Akayesu*, Trial Chamber I expanded the Genocide Convention and Tribunal Statute and introduced a subjective standard for determining what groups in a particular society are protected by the Genocide Convention. Arguably, by definition there would have been no genocide in Rwanda had Chamber not done this. In addition, the chamber explicated a method for determining an individual's constructive genocidal intent. It also offered definitions of rape and sexual violence for purposes of humanitarian law. Trial Chamber I's lengthy judgment carefully explicates the facts, reasoning, and rules it relied upon to reach its conclusions. By so doing, the *Akayesu* Judgment will stand as an historic precedent for future tribunals dealing with similar issues.

Countering the ICTR's achievements has been its slowness in prosecuting the more than thirty people in custody at the start of 1999. If it proceeds at its past pace, many of these indictees will remain in detention for several years before their cases are heard. The creation of a third trial chamber in 1999 will help, but further efficiencies in operations and procedures are needed. For the ICTR to administer justice fairly and promptly, it must function more efficiently.

It must be stressed, however, that the judges and many of the ICTR's staff have worked with great dedication and courage under difficult conditions to accomplish an important humanitarian goal. As we move past the fiftieth anniversary of the Universal Declaration of Human Rights, we must recognize that the ICTR is a significant step towards ending the culture of impunity. It has already contributed to the jurisprudence of the future International Criminal Court.

The twentieth century will be remembered both for its barbaric acts and for its affirmation of the fundamental principles of human rights and international humanitarian law. Hopefully, the twenty-first century will effectively implement these principles. The ICTR and the ICTY have already influenced the way many states view the causes of grave humanitarian crimes and possible strategies for achieving peace and national reconciliation.

Appendix A

United Nations Security Council Resolution 955 with the Statute of the
International Tribunal for Rwanda Annexed

S/RES/955 (1994)
8 November 1994

RESOLUTION 955 (1994)
Adopted by the Security Council at its 3453rd meeting, on 8 November 1994

The Security Council,
Reaffirming all its previous resolutions on the situation in Rwanda,

Having considered the reports of the Secretary-General pursuant to paragraph 3 of resolution 935 (1994) of 1 July 1994 (S/1994/879 and S/1994/906), and having taken note of the reports of the Special Rapporteur for Rwanda of the United Nations Commission on Human Rights (S/1994/1157, annex I and annex II),

Expressing appreciation for the work of the Commission of Experts established pursuant to resolution 935 (1994), in particular its preliminary report on violations of international humanitarian law in Rwanda transmitted by the Secretary-General's letter of 1 October 1994 (S/1994/1125),

Expressing once again its grave concern at the reports indicating that genocide and other systematic, widespread and flagrant violations of international humanitarian law have been committed in Rwanda,

Determining that this situation continues to constitute a threat to international peace and security,

Determined to put an end to such crimes and to take effective measures to bring to justice the persons who are responsible for them,

Convinced that in the particular circumstances of Rwanda, the prosecution of persons responsible for serious violations of international humanitarian law would enable this aim to be achieved and would contribute to the process of national reconciliation and to the restoration and maintenance of peace,

Believing that the establishment of an international tribunal for the prosecution of persons responsible for genocide and the other above-mentioned violations of international humanitarian law will contribute to ensuring that such violations are halted and effectively redressed,

Stressing also the need for international cooperation to strengthen the courts and judicial system of Rwanda, having regard in particular to the necessity for those courts to deal with large numbers of suspects,

Considering that the Commission of Experts established pursuant to resolution 935 (1994) should continue on an urgent basis the collection of information relating to evidence of grave violations of international humanitarian law committed in the territory of Rwanda and should submit its final report to the Secretary-General by 30 November 1994,

Acting under Chapter VII of the Charter of the United Nations,

1. Decides hereby, having received the request of the Government of Rwanda (S/1994/1115), to establish an international tribunal for the sole purpose of prosecuting persons responsible for genocide and other serious violations of international humanitarian law committed in the territory of Rwanda and Rwandan citizens responsible for genocide and other such violations committed in the territory of neighbouring States, between 1 January 1994 and 31 December 1994 and to this end to adopt the Statute of the International Criminal Tribunal for Rwanda annexed hereto;

2. Decides that all States shall cooperate fully with the International Tribunal and its organs in accordance with the present resolution and the Statute of the International Tribunal and that consequently all States shall take any measures necessary under their domestic law to implement the provisions of the present resolution and the Statute, including the obligation of States to comply with requests for assistance or orders issued by a Trial Chamber under Article 28 of the Statute, and requests States to keep the Secretary-General informed of such measures;

3. Considers that the Government of Rwanda should be notified prior to the taking of decisions under articles 26 and 27 of the Statute;

4. Urges States and intergovernmental and non-governmental organizations to contribute funds, equipment and services to the International Tribunal, including the offer of expert personnel;

5. Requests the Secretary-General to implement this resolution urgently and in particular to make practical arrangements for the effective functioning of the International Tribunal, including recommendations to the Council as to possible locations for the seat of the International Tribunal at the earliest time and to report periodically to the Council;

6. Decides that the seat of the International Tribunal shall be determined by the Council having regard to considerations of justice and fairness as well as administrative efficiency, including access to witnesses, and economy, and subject to the conclusion of appropriate arrangements between the United Nations and the State of the seat, acceptable to the Council, having regard to the fact that the International Tribunal may meet away from its seat when it considers it necessary for the efficient exercise of its functions; and decides that an office will be established and proceedings will be conducted in Rwanda, where feasible and appropriate, subject to the conclusion of similar appropriate arrangements;

7. Decides to consider increasing the number of judges and Trial Chambers of the International Tribunal if it becomes necessary;

8. Decides to remain actively seized of the matter.

Annex

Statute of the International Tribunal for Rwanda

Having been established by the Security Council acting under Chapter VII of the Charter of the United Nations, the International Criminal Tribunal for the Prosecution of Persons Responsible for Genocide and Other Serious Violations of International Humanitarian Law Committed in the Territory of Rwanda and Rwandan citizens responsible for genocide and other such violations committed in the territory of neighbouring States, between 1 January 1994 and 31 December 1994 (hereinafter referred to as 'the International Tribunal for Rwanda') shall function in accordance with the provisions of the present Statute.

Article 1
Competence of the International Tribunal for Rwanda

The International Tribunal for Rwanda shall have the power to prosecute persons responsible for serious violations of international humanitarian law committed in the territory of Rwanda and Rwandan citizens responsible for such violations committed in the territory of neighbouring States, between 1 January 1994 and 31 December 1994, in accordance with the provisions of the present Statute.

Article 2
Genocide

1. The International Tribunal for Rwanda shall have the power to prosecute persons committing genocide as defined in paragraph 2 of this article or of committing any of the other acts enumerated in paragraph 3 of this article.

2. Genocide means any of the following acts committed with intent to destroy, in whole or in part, a national, ethnical, racial or religious group, as such:

(a) Killing members of the group;

(b) Causing serious bodily or mental harm to members of the group;

(c) Deliberately inflicting on the group conditions of life calculated to bring about its physical destruction in whole or in part;

(d) Imposing measures intended to prevent births within the group;

(e) Forcibly transferring children of the group to another group.

3. The following acts shall be punishable:

(a) Genocide;

(b) Conspiracy to commit genocide;

(c) Direct and public incitement to commit genocide;

(d) Attempt to commit genocide;

(e) Complicity in genocide.

Article 3
Crimes against humanity

The International Tribunal for Rwanda shall have the power to prosecute persons responsible for the following crimes when committed as part of a widespread or systematic attack against any civilian population on national, political, ethnic, racial or religious grounds:

(a) Murder;

(b) Extermination;

(c) Enslavement;

(d) Deportation;

(e) Imprisonment;

(f) Torture;

(g) Rape;

(h) Persecutions on political, racial and religious grounds;

(i) Other inhumane acts.

Article 4
Violations of Article 3 common to the Geneva Conventions and of Additional Protocol II

The International Tribunal for Rwanda shall have the power to prosecute persons committing or ordering to be committed serious violations of Article 3 common to the Geneva Conventions of 12 August 1949 for the Protection of War Victims, and of Additional Protocol II thereto of 8 June 1977. These violations shall include, but shall not be limited to:

(a) Violence to life, health and physical or mental well-being of persons, in particular murder as well as cruel treatment such as torture, mutilation or any form of corporal punishment;

(b) Collective punishments;

(c) Taking of hostages;

(d) Acts of terrorism;

(e) Outrages upon personal dignity, in particular humiliating and degrading treatment, rape, enforced prostitution and any form of indecent assault;

(f) Pillage;

(g) The passing of sentences and the carrying out of executions without previous judgement pronounced by a regularly constituted court, affording all the judicial guarantees which are recognized as indispensable by civilized peoples;

(h) Threats to commit any of the foregoing acts.

Article 5
Personal jurisdiction

The International Tribunal for Rwanda shall have jurisdiction over natural persons pursuant to the provisions of the present Statute.

Article 6
Individual criminal responsibility

1. A person who planned, instigated, ordered, committed or otherwise aided and abetted in the planning, preparation or execution of a crime referred to in articles 2 to 4 of the present Statute, shall be individually responsible for the crime.

2. The official position of any accused person, whether as Head of State or Government or as a responsible Government official, shall not relieve such person of criminal responsibility nor mitigate punishment.

3. The fact that any of the acts referred to in articles 2 to 4 of the present Statute was committed by a subordinate does not relieve his or her superior of criminal responsibility if he or she knew or had reason to know that the subordinate was about to commit such acts or had done so and the superior failed to take the necessary and reasonable measures to prevent such acts or to punish the perpetrators thereof.

4. The fact that an accused person acted pursuant to an order of a Government or of a superior shall not relieve him or her of criminal responsibility, but may be considered in mitigation of punishment if the International Tribunal for Rwanda determines that justice so requires.

Article 7
Territorial and temporal jurisdiction

The territorial jurisdiction of the International Tribunal for Rwanda shall extend to the territory of Rwanda including its land surface and airspace as well as to the territory of neighbouring States in respect of serious violations of international humanitarian law committed by Rwandan citizens. The temporal jurisdiction of the International Tribunal for Rwanda shall extend to a period beginning on 1 January 1994 and ending on 31 December 1994.

Article 8
Concurrent jurisdiction

1. The International Tribunal for Rwanda and national courts shall have concurrent

jurisdiction to prosecute persons for serious violations of international humanitarian law committed in the territory of Rwanda and Rwandan citizens for such violations committed in the territory of neighbouring States, between 1 January 1994 and 31 December 1994.

2. The International Tribunal for Rwanda shall have primacy over the national courts of all States. At any stage of the procedure, the International Tribunal for Rwanda may formally request national courts to defer to its competence in accordance with the present Statute and the Rules of Procedure and Evidence of the International Tribunal for Rwanda.

Article 9
Non bis in idem

1. No person shall be tried before a national court for acts constituting serious violations of international humanitarian law under the present Statute, for which he or she has already been tried by the International Tribunal for Rwanda.

2. A person who has been tried by a national court for acts constituting serious violations of international humanitarian law may be subsequently tried by the International Tribunal for Rwanda only if:

(a) The act for which he or she was tried was characterized as an ordinary crime; or

(b) The national court proceedings were not impartial or independent, were designed to shield the accused from international criminal responsibility, or the case was not diligently prosecuted.

3. In considering the penalty to be imposed on a person convicted of a crime under the present Statute, the International Tribunal for Rwanda shall take into account the extent to which any penalty imposed by a national court on the same person for the same act has already been served.

Article 10
Organization of the International Tribunal for Rwanda

The International Tribunal for Rwanda shall consist of the following organs:

(a) The Chambers, comprising two Trial Chambers and an Appeals Chamber;

(b) The Prosecutor; and

(c) A Registry.

Article 11
Composition of the Chambers

The Chambers shall be composed of eleven independent judges, no two of whom may be nationals of the same State, who shall serve as follows:

(a) Three judges shall serve in each of the Trial Chambers;

(b) Five judges shall serve in the Appeals Chamber.

Article 12
Qualification and election of judges

1. The judges shall be persons of high moral character, impartiality and integrity who possess the qualifications required in their respective countries for appointment to the highest judicial offices. In the overall composition of the Chambers due account shall be taken of the experience of the judges in criminal law, international law, including international humanitarian law and human rights law.

2. The members of the Appeals Chamber of the International Tribunal for the Prosecution of Persons Responsible for Serious Violations of International Law Committed in the Territory of the Former Yugoslavia since 1991 (hereinafter referred to as 'the International Tribunal for the Former Yugoslavia') shall also serve as the members of the Appeals Chamber of the International Tribunal for Rwanda.

3. The judges of the Trial Chambers of the International Tribunal for Rwanda shall be elected by the General Assembly from a list submitted by the Security Council, in the following manner:

(a) The Secretary-General shall invite nominations for judges of the Trial Chambers from States Members of the United Nations and non-member States maintaining permanent observer missions at United Nations Headquarters;

(b) Within thirty days of the date of the invitation of the Secretary-General, each State may nominate up to two candidates meeting the qualifications set out in paragraph 1 above, no two of whom shall be of the same nationality and neither of whom shall be of the same nationality as any judge on the Appeals Chamber;

(c) The Secretary-General shall forward the nominations received to the Security Council. From the nominations received the Security Council shall establish a list of not less than twelve and not more than eighteen candidates, taking due account of adequate representation on the International Tribunal for Rwanda of the principal legal systems of the world;

(d) The President of the Security Council shall transmit the list of candidates to the President of the General Assembly. From that list the General Assembly shall elect the six judges of the Trial Chambers. The candidates who receive an absolute majority of the votes of the States Members of the United Nations and of the non-Member States maintaining permanent observer missions at United Nations Headquarters, shall be declared elected. Should two candidates of the same nationality obtain the required majority vote, the one who received the higher number of votes shall be considered elected.

4. In the event of a vacancy in the Trial Chambers, after consultation with the Presidents of the Security Council and of the General Assembly, the Secretary-General shall appoint a person meeting the qualifications of paragraph 1 above, for the remainder of the term of office concerned.

5. The judges of the Trial Chambers shall be elected for a term of four years. The terms and conditions of service shall be those of the judges of the International Tribunal for the Former Yugoslavia. They shall be eligible for re-election.

Article 13
Officers and members of the Chambers

1. The judges of the International Tribunal for Rwanda shall elect a President.

2. After consultation with the judges of the International Tribunal for Rwanda, the President shall assign the judges to the Trial Chambers. A judge shall serve only in the Chamber to which he or she was assigned.

3. The judges of each Trial Chamber shall elect a Presiding Judge, who shall conduct all of the proceedings of that Trial Chamber as a whole.

Article 14
Rules of procedure and evidence

The judges of the International Tribunal for Rwanda shall adopt, for the purpose of proceedings before the International Tribunal for Rwanda, the rules of procedure and evidence for the conduct of the pre-trial phase of the proceedings, trials and appeals, the admission of evidence, the protection of victims and witnesses and other appropriate matters of the International Tribunal for the Former Yugoslavia with such changes as they deem necessary.

Article 15
The Prosecutor

1. The Prosecutor shall be responsible for the investigation and prosecution of persons

responsible for serious violations of international humanitarian law committed in the territory of Rwanda and Rwandan citizens responsible for such violations committed in the territory of neighbouring States, between 1 January 1994 and 31 December 1994.

2. The Prosecutor shall act independently as a separate organ of the International Tribunal for Rwanda. He or she shall not seek or receive instructions from any Government or from any other source.

3. The Prosecutor of the International Tribunal for the Former Yugoslavia shall also serve as the Prosecutor of the International Tribunal for Rwanda. He or she shall have additional staff, including an additional Deputy Prosecutor, to assist with prosecutions before the International Tribunal for Rwanda. Such staff shall be appointed by the Secretary-General on the recommendation of the Prosecutor.

Article 16
The Registry

1. The Registry shall be responsible for the administration and servicing of the International Tribunal for Rwanda.

2. The Registry shall consist of a Registrar and such other staff as may be required.

3. The Registrar shall be appointed by the Secretary-General after consultation with the President of the International Tribunal for Rwanda. He or she shall serve for a four-year term and be eligible for reappointment. The terms and conditions of service of the Registrar shall be those of an Assistant Secretary-General of the United Nations.

4. The staff of the Registry shall be appointed by the Secretary-General on the recommendation of the Registrar.

Article 17
Investigation and preparation of indictment

1. The Prosecutor shall initiate investigations ex-officio or on the basis of information obtained from any source, particularly from Governments, United Nations organs, intergovernmental and non-governmental organizations.

The Prosecutor shall assess the information received or obtained and decide whether there is sufficient basis to proceed.

2. The Prosecutor shall have the power to question suspects, victims and witnesses, to collect evidence and to conduct on-site investigations. In carrying out these tasks, the Prosecutor may, as appropriate, seek the assistance of the State authorities concerned.

3. If questioned, the suspect shall be entitled to be assisted by counsel of his or her own choice, including the right to have legal assistance assigned to the suspect without payment by him or her in any such case if he or she does not have sufficient means to pay for it, as well as to necessary translation into and from a language he or she speaks and understands.

4. Upon a determination that a prima facie case exists, the Prosecutor shall prepare an indictment containing a concise statement of the facts and the crime or crimes with which the accused is charged under the Statute. The indictment shall be transmitted to a judge of the Trial Chamber.

Article 18
Review of the indictment

1. The judge of the Trial Chamber to whom the indictment has been transmitted shall review it. If satisfied that a prima facie case has been established by the Prosecutor, he or she shall confirm the indictment. If not so satisfied, the indictment shall be dismissed.

2. Upon confirmation of an indictment, the judge may, at the request of the Prosecutor, issue such orders and warrants for the arrest, detention, surrender or transfer of persons, and any other orders as may be required for the conduct of the trial.

Article 19
Commencement and conduct of trial proceedings

1. The Trial Chambers shall ensure that a trial is fair and expeditious and that proceedings are conducted in accordance with the rules of procedure and evidence, with full respect for the rights of the accused and due regard for the protection of victims and witnesses.

2. A person against whom an indictment has been confirmed shall, pursuant to an order or an arrest warrant of the International Tribunal for Rwanda, be taken into custody, immediately informed of the charges against him or her and transferred to the International Tribunal for Rwanda.

3. The Trial Chamber shall read the indictment, satisfy itself that the rights of the accused are respected, confirm that the accused understands the indictment, and instruct the accused to enter a plea. The Trial Chamber shall then set the date for trial.

4. The hearings shall be public unless the Trial Chamber decides to close the proceedings in accordance with its rules of procedure and evidence.

Article 20
Rights of the accused

1. All persons shall be equal before the International Tribunal for Rwanda.

2. In the determination of charges against him or her, the accused shall be entitled to a fair and public hearing, subject to article 21 of the Statute.

3. The accused shall be presumed innocent until proved guilty according to the provisions of the present Statute.

4. In the determination of any charge against the accused pursuant to the present Statute, the accused shall be entitled to the following minimum guarantees, in full equality:

(a) To be informed promptly and in detail in a language which he or she understands of the nature and cause of the charge against him or her;

(b) To have adequate time and facilities for the preparation of his or her defence and to communicate with counsel of his or her own choosing;

(c) To be tried without undue delay;

(d) To be tried in his or her presence, and to defend himself or herself in person or through legal assistance of his or her own choosing; to be informed, if he or she does not have legal assistance, of this right; and to have legal assistance assigned to him or her, in any case where the interests of justice so require, and without payment by him or her in any such case if he or she does not have sufficient means to pay for it;

(e) To examine, or have examined, the witnesses against him or her and to obtain the attendance and examination of witnesses on his or her behalf under the same conditions as witnesses against him or her;

(f) To have the free assistance of an interpreter if he or she cannot understand or speak the language used in the International Tribunal for Rwanda;

(g) Not to be compelled to testify against himself or herself or to confess guilt.

Article 21
Protection of victims and witnesses

The International Tribunal for Rwanda shall provide in its rules of procedure and evidence for the protection of victims and witnesses. Such protection measures shall include, but shall not be limited to, the conduct of in camera proceedings and the protection of the victim's identity.

Article 22
Judgement

1. The Trial Chambers shall pronounce judgements and impose sentences and penalties on persons convicted of serious violations of international humanitarian law.

2. The judgement shall be rendered by a majority of the judges of the Trial Chamber, and shall be delivered by the Trial Chamber in public. It shall be accompanied by a reasoned opinion in writing, to which separate or dissenting opinions may be appended.

Article 23
Penalties

1. The penalty imposed by the Trial Chamber shall be limited to imprisonment. In determining the terms of imprisonment, the Trial Chambers shall have recourse to the general practice regarding prison sentences in the courts of Rwanda.

2. In imposing the sentences, the Trial Chambers should take into account such factors as the gravity of the offence and the individual circumstances of the convicted person.

3. In addition to imprisonment, the Trial Chambers may order the return of any property and proceeds acquired by criminal conduct, including by means of duress, to their rightful owners.

Article 24
Appellate proceedings

1. The Appeals Chamber shall hear appeals from persons convicted by the Trial Chambers or from the Prosecutor on the following grounds:

(a) An error on a question of law invalidating the decision; or

(b) An error of fact which has occasioned a miscarriage of justice.

2. The Appeals Chamber may affirm, reverse or revise the decisions taken by the Trial Chambers.

Article 25
Review proceedings

Where a new fact has been discovered which was not known at the time of the proceedings before the Trial Chambers or the Appeals Chamber and which could have been a decisive factor in reaching the decision, the convicted person or the Prosecutor may submit to the International Tribunal for Rwanda an application for review of the judgement.

Article 26
Enforcement of sentences

Imprisonment shall be served in Rwanda or any of the States on a list of States which have indicated to the Security Council their willingness to accept convicted persons, as designated by the International Tribunal for Rwanda. Such imprisonment shall be in accordance with the applicable law of the State concerned, subject to the supervision of the International Tribunal for Rwanda.

Article 27
Pardon or commutation of sentences

If, pursuant to the applicable law of the State in which the convicted person is imprisoned, he or she is eligible for pardon or commutation of sentence, the State concerned shall notify the International Tribunal for Rwanda accordingly. There shall only be pardon or commutation of sentence if the President of the International Tribunal for Rwanda, in consultation with the judges, so decides on the basis of the interests of justice and the general principles of law.

Article 28
Cooperation and judicial assistance

1. States shall cooperate with the International Tribunal for Rwanda in the investigation and prosecution of persons accused of committing serious violations of international humanitarian law.

2. States shall comply without undue delay with any request for assistance or an order issued by a Trial Chamber, including, but not limited to:

(a) The identification and location of persons;

(b) The taking of testimony and the production of evidence;

(c) The service of documents;

(d) The arrest or detention of persons;

(e) The surrender or the transfer of the accused to the International Tribunal for Rwanda.

Article 29
The status, privileges and immunities of the International Tribunal for Rwanda

1. The Convention on the Privileges and Immunities of the United Nations of 13 February 1946 shall apply to the International Tribunal for Rwanda, the judges, the Prosecutor and his or her staff, and the Registrar and his or her staff.

2. The judges, the Prosecutor and the Registrar shall enjoy the privileges and immunities, exemptions and facilities accorded to diplomatic envoys, in accordance with international law.

3. The staff of the Prosecutor and of the Registrar shall enjoy the privileges and immunities accorded to officials of the United Nations under articles V and VII of the Convention referred to in paragraph 1 of this article.

4. Other persons, including the accused, required at the seat or meeting place of the International Tribunal for Rwanda shall be accorded such treatment as is necessary for the proper functioning of the International Tribunal for Rwanda.

Article 30
Expenses of the International Tribunal for Rwanda

The expenses of the International Tribunal for Rwanda shall be expenses of the Organization in accordance with Article 17 of the Charter of the United Nations.

Article 31
Working languages

The working languages of the International Tribunal shall be English and French.

Article 32
Annual report

The President of the International Tribunal for Rwanda shall submit an annual report of the International Tribunal for Rwanda to the Security Council and to the General Assembly.

[See Appendix B for amendments.]

Appendix B

United Nations Security Council Resolution 1165 (30 April 1998)

AMENDMENTS TO THE STATUTE OF THE INTERNATIONAL TRIBUNAL FOR RWANDA

Article 10
Organization of the International Tribunal for Rwanda

The International Tribunal for Rwanda shall consist of the following organs:

(a) The Chambers, comprising three Trial Chambers and an Appeals Chamber;

(b) The Prosecutor;

(c) A Registry.

Article 11
Composition of the Chambers

The Chambers shall be composed of fourteen independent judges, no two of whom may be nationals of the same State, who shall serve as follows:

(a) Three judges shall serve in each of the Trial Chambers;

(b) Five judges shall serve in the Appeals Chamber.

Article 12
Qualification and election of judges

1. The judges shall be persons of high moral character, impartiality and integrity who possess the qualifications required in their respective countries for appointment to the highest judicial offices. In the overall composition of the Chambers due account shall

be taken of the experience of the judges in criminal law, international law, including international humanitarian law and human rights law.

2. The members of the Appeals Chamber of the International Tribunal for the Prosecution of Persons Responsible for Serious Violations of International Humanitarian Law Committed in the Territory of the Former Yugoslavia since 1991 (hereinafter referred to as 'the International Tribunal for the Former Yugoslavia') shall also serve as the members of the Appeals Chamber of the International Tribunal for Rwanda.

3. The judges of the Trial Chambers of the International Tribunal for Rwanda shall be elected by the General Assembly from a list submitted by the Security Council, in the following manner:

(a) The Secretary-General shall invite nominations for judges of the Trial Chambers from States Members of the United Nations and non-member States maintaining permanent observer missions at United Nations Headquarters;

(b) Within thirty days of the date of the invitation of the Secretary-General, each State may nominate up to two candidates meeting the qualifications set out in paragraph 1 above, no two of whom shall be of the same nationality and neither of whom shall be of the same nationality as any judge on the Appeals Chamber;

(c) The Secretary-General shall forward the nominations received to the Security Council. From the nominations received, the Security Council shall establish a list of not less than eighteen and not more than twenty-seven candidates, taking due account of adequate representation on the International Tribunal for Rwanda of the principal legal systems of the world;

(d) The President of the Security Council shall transmit the list of candidates to the President of the General Assembly. From that list, the General Assembly shall elect the nine judges of the Trial Chambers. The candidates who receive an absolute majority of the votes of the States Members of the United Nations and of the non-member States maintaining permanent observer missions at United Nations Headquarters shall be declared elected. Should two candidates of the same nationality obtain the required majority vote, the one who received the higher number of votes shall be considered elected.

4. In the event of a vacancy in the Trial Chambers, after consultation with the Presidents of the Security Council and the General Assembly, the Secretary-General shall appoint a person meeting the qualifications of paragraph 1 above, for the remainder of the term of office concerned.

5. The judges of the Trial Chambers shall be elected for a term of four years. The terms and conditions of service shall be those of the judges of the International Tribunal for the Former Yugoslavia. They shall be eligible for re-election.

Appendix C

THE INTERNATIONAL CRIMINAL TRIBUNAL FOR RWANDA

CASE NO: ICTR-96-4-I

THE PROSECUTOR OF THE TRIBUNAL

AGAINST

JEAN PAUL AKAYESU

AMENDED INDICTMENT

The Prosecutor of the International Criminal Tribunal for Rwanda, pursuant to his authority under Article 17 of the Statute of the Tribunal, charges:

JEAN PAUL AKAYESU

with GENOCIDE, CRIMES AGAINST HUMANITY and VIOLATIONS OF ARTICLE 3 COMMON TO THE GENEVA CONVENTIONS, as set forth below:

Background

1. On April 6, 1994, a plane carrying President Juvénal Habyarimana of Rwanda and President Cyprien Ntaryamira of Burundi crashed at Kigali airport, killing all on board. Following the deaths of the two Presidents, widespread killings, having both political and ethnic dimensions, began in Kigali and spread to other parts of Rwanda.

2. Rwanda is divided into 11 prefectures, each of which is governed by a prefect. The prefectures are further subdivided into communes which are placed under the authority of bourgmestres. The bourgmestre of each commune is appointed by the President of the Republic, upon the recommendation of the Minister of the Interior. In Rwanda, the

bourgmestre is the most powerful figure in the commune. His de facto authority in the area is significantly greater than that which is conferred upon him de jure.

The Accused

3. Jean Paul AKAYESU, born in 1953 in Murehe sector, Taba commune, served as bourgmestre of that commune from April 1993 until June 1994. Prior to his appointment as bourgmestre, he was a teacher and school inspector in Taba.

4. As bourgmestre, Jean Paul AKAYESU was charged with the performance of executive functions and the maintenance of public order within his commune, subject to the authority of the prefect. He had exclusive control over the communal police, as well as any gendarmes put at the disposition of the commune. He was responsible for the execution of laws and regulations and the administration of justice, also subject only to the prefect's authority.

General Allegations

5. Unless otherwise specified, all acts and omissions set forth in this indictment took place between 1 January 1994 and 31 December 1994, in the commune of Taba, prefecture of Gitarama, territory of Rwanda.

6. In each paragraph charging genocide, a crime recognized by Article 2 of the Statute of the Tribunal, the alleged acts or omissions were committed with intent to destroy, in whole or in part, a national, ethnic or racial group.

7. The victims in each paragraph charging genocide were members of a national, ethnic, racial or religious group.

8. In each paragraph charging crimes against humanity, crimes recognized by Article 3 of the Tribunal Statute, the alleged acts or omissions were committed as part of a widespread or systematic attack against a civilian population on national, political, ethnic or racial grounds.

9. At all times relevant to this indictment, a state of internal armed conflict existed in Rwanda.

10. The victims referred to in this indictment were, at all relevant times, persons not taking an active part in the hostilities.

10A. In this indictment, acts of sexual violence include forcible sexual penetration of the vagina, anus or oral cavity by a penis and/or of the vagina or anus by some other object, and sexual abuse, such as forced nudity.

11. The accused is individually responsible for the crimes alleged in this indictment. Under Article 6(1) of the Statute of the Tribunal, individual criminal responsibility is attributable to one who plans, instigates, orders, commits or otherwise aids and abets in the planning, preparation or execution of any of the crimes referred to in Articles 2 to 4 of the Statute of the Tribunal.

Charges

12. As bourgmestre, Jean Paul AKAYESU was responsible for maintaining law and public order in his commune. At least 2000 Tutsis were killed in Taba between April 7 and the end of June, 1994, while he was still in power. The killings in Taba were openly committed and so widespread that, as bourgmestre, Jean Paul AKAYESU must have known about them. Although he had the authority and responsibility to do so, Jean Paul AKAYESU never attempted to prevent the killing of Tutsis in the commune in any way or called for assistance from regional or national authorities to quell the violence.

12A. Between April 7 and the end of June, 1994, hundreds of civilians (hereinafter "displaced civilians") sought refuge at the bureau communal. The majority of these displaced civilians were Tutsi. While seeking refuge at the bureau communal, female displaced civilians were regularly taken by armed local militia and/or communal police and subjected to sexual violence, and/or beaten on or near the bureau communal premises. Displaced civilians were also murdered frequently on or near the bureau communal premises. Many women were forced to endure multiple acts of sexual violence which were at times committed by more than one assailant. These acts of sexual violence were generally accompanied by explicit threats of death or bodily harm. The female displaced civilians lived in constant fear and their physical and psychological health deteriorated as a result of the sexual violence and beatings and killings.

12B. Jean Paul AKAYESU knew that the acts of sexual violence, beatings and murders were being committed and was at times present during their commission. Jean Paul AKAYESU facilitated the commission of the sexual violence, beatings and murders by allowing the sexual violence and beatings and murders to occur on or near the bureau communal premises. By virtue of his presence during the commission of the sexual violence, beatings and murders and by failing to prevent the sexual violence, beatings and murders, Jean Paul AKAYESU encouraged these activities.

13. On or about 19 April 1994, before dawn, in Gishyeshye sector, Taba commune, a group of men, one of whom was named Francois Ndimubanzi, killed a local teacher, Sylvere Karera, because he was accused of associating with the Rwandan Patriotic Front ('RPF') and plotting to kill Hutus. Even though at least one of the perpetrators was turned over to Jean Paul AKAYESU, he failed to take measures to have him arrested.

14. The morning of April 19, 1994, following the murder of Sylvere Karera, Jean Paul AKAYESU led a meeting in Gishyeshye sector at which he sanctioned the death of

Sylvere Karera and urged the population to eliminate accomplices of the RPF, which was understood by those present to mean Tutsis. Over 100 people were present at the meeting. The killing of Tutsis in Taba began shortly after the meeting.

15. At the same meeting in Gishyeshye sector on April 19, 1994, Jean Paul AKAYESU named at least three prominent Tutsis–Ephrem Karangwa, Juvénal Rukundakuvuga and Emmanuel Sempabwa–who had to be killed because of their alleged relationships with the RPF. Later that day, Juvénal Rukundakuvuga was killed in Kanyinya. Within the next few days, Emmanuel Sempabwa was clubbed to death in front of the Taba bureau communal.

16. Jean Paul AKAYESU, on or about April 19, 1994, conducted house-to-house searches in Taba. During these searches, residents, including Victim V, were interrogated and beaten with rifles and sticks in the presence of Jean Paul AKAYESU. Jean Paul AKAYESU personally threatened to kill the husband and child of Victim U if she did not provide him with information about the activities of the Tutsis he was seeking.

17. On or about April 19, 1994, Jean Paul AKAYESU ordered the interrogation and beating of Victim X in an effort to learn the whereabouts of Ephrem Karangwa. During the beating, Victim X's fingers were broken as he tried to shield himself from blows with a metal stick.

18. On or about April 19, 1994, the men who, on Jean Paul AKAYESU's instructions, were searching for Ephrem Karangwa destroyed Ephrem Karangwa's house and burned down his mother's house. They then went to search the house of Ephrem Karangwa's brother-in-law in Musambira commune and found Ephrem Karangwa's three brothers there. The three brothers–Simon Mutijima, Thaddée Uwanyiligira and Jean Chrysostome Gakuba–tried to escape, but Jean Paul AKAYESU blew his whistle to alert local residents to the attempted escape and ordered the people to capture the brothers. After the brothers were captured, Jean Paul AKAYESU ordered and participated in the killings of the three brothers.

19. On or about April 19, 1994, Jean Paul AKAYESU took 8 detained men from the Taba bureau communal and ordered militia members to kill them. The militia killed them with clubs, machetes, small axes and sticks. The victims had fled from Runda commune and had been held by Jean Paul AKAYESU.

20. On or about April 19, 1994, Jean Paul AKAYESU ordered the local people and militia to kill intellectual and influential people. Five teachers from the secondary school of Taba were killed on his instructions. The victims were Theogene, Phoebe Uwineze and her fiancé (whose name is unknown), Tharcisse Twizeyumuremye and Samuel. The local people and militia killed them with machetes and agricultural tools in front of the Taba bureau communal.

21. On or about April 20, 1994, Jean Paul AKAYESU and some communal police went to the house of Victim Y, a 68 year old woman. Jean Paul AKAYESU interrogated her about the whereabouts of the wife of a university teacher. During the questioning, under Jean Paul AKAYESU's supervision, the communal police hit Victim Y with a gun and sticks. They bound her arms and legs and repeatedly kicked her in the chest. Jean Paul AKAYESU threatened to kill her if she failed to provide the information he sought.

22. Later that night, on or about April 20, 1994, Jean Paul AKAYESU picked up Victim W in Taba and interrogated her also about the whereabouts of the wife of the university teacher. When she stated she did not know, he forced her to lay on the road in front of his car and threatened to drive over her.

23. Thereafter, on or about April 20, 1994, Jean Paul AKAYESU picked up Victim Z in Taba and interrogated him. During the interrogation, men under Jean Paul AKAYESU's authority forced Victims Z and Y to beat each other and used a piece of Victim Y's dress to strangle Victim Z.

Counts 1-3
(Genocide)
(Crimes against Humanity)

By his acts in relation to the events described in paragraphs 12-23, Jean Paul AKAYESU is criminally responsible for:

COUNT 1: GENOCIDE, punishable by Article 2(3)(a) of the Statute of the Tribunal;

COUNT 2: Complicity in GENOCIDE, punishable by Article 2(3)(e) of the Statute of the Tribunal; and

COUNT 3: CRIMES AGAINST HUMANITY (extermination), punishable by Article 3(b) of the Statute of the Tribunal.

Count 4
(Incitement to Commit Genocide)

By his acts in relation to the events described in paragraphs 14 and 15, Jean Paul AKAYESU is criminally responsible for:

COUNT 4: Direct and Public Incitement to Commit GENOCIDE, punishable by Article 2(3)(c) of the Statute of the Tribunal.

Counts 5-6
(Crimes Against Humanity)
(Violations of Article 3 common to the Geneva Conventions)

By his acts in relation the murders of Juvénal Rukundakuvuga, Emmanuel Sempabwa, Simon Mutijima, Thaddée Uwanyiligira and Jean Chrysostome Gakuba, as described in paragraphs 15 and 18, Jean Paul AKAYESU committed:

COUNT 5: CRIMES AGAINST HUMANITY (murder) punishable by Article 3(a) of the Statute of the Tribunal; and

COUNT 6: VIOLATIONS OF ARTICLE 3 COMMON TO THE GENEVA CONVENTIONS, as incorporated by Article 4(a)(murder) of the Statute of the Tribunal.

Counts 7-8
(Crimes Against Humanity)
(Violations of Article 3 common to the Geneva Conventions)

By his acts in relation the murders of 8 detained men in front of the bureau communal as described in paragraph 19, Jean Paul AKAYESU committed:

COUNT 7: CRIMES AGAINST HUMANITY (murder) punishable by Article 3(a) of the Statute of the Tribunal; and

COUNT 8: VIOLATIONS OF ARTICLE 3 COMMON TO THE GENEVA CONVENTIONS, as incorporated by Article 4(a)(murder) of the Statute of the Tribunal.

Counts 9-10
(Crimes Against Humanity)
(Violations of Article 3 common to the Geneva Conventions)

By his acts in relation to the murders of 5 teachers in front of the bureau communal as described in paragraph 20, Jean Paul AKAYESU committed:

COUNT 9: CRIMES AGAINST HUMANITY (murder) punishable by Article 3(a) of the Statute of the Tribunal; and

COUNT 10: VIOLATIONS OF ARTICLE 3 COMMON TO THE GENEVA CONVENTIONS, as incorporated by Article 4(a)(murder) of the Statute of the Tribunal.

Counts 11-12
(Crimes Against Humanity)
(Violations of Article 3 common to the Geneva Conventions)

By his acts in relation to the beatings of U, V, W, X, Y and Z as described in paragraphs 16, 17, 21, 22 and 23, Jean Paul AKAYESU committed:

COUNT 11: CRIMES AGAINST HUMANITY (torture), punishable by Article 3(f) of the Statute of the Tribunal; and

COUNT 12: VIOLATIONS OF ARTICLE 3 COMMON TO THE GENEVA CONVENTIONS, as incorporated by Article 4(a)(cruel treatment) of the Statute of the Tribunal.

In addition and/or in the alternative to his individual responsibility under Article 6(1) of the Statute of the Tribunal, the accused, is individually responsible under Article 6(3) of the Statute of the Tribunal for the crimes alleged in Counts 13 through 15. Under Article 6(3), an individual is criminally responsible as a superior for acts of a subordinate if he or she knew or had reason to know that the subordinate was about to commit such acts or had done so and the superior failed to take the necessary and reasonable measures to prevent such acts or to punish the perpetrators thereof.

Counts 13-15
(Crimes Against Humanity)
(Violations of Article 3 common to the Geneva Conventions)

By his acts in relation to the events at the bureau communal, as described in paragraphs 12(A) and 12(B), Jean Paul AKAYESU committed:

COUNT 13: CRIMES AGAINST HUMANITY (rape), punishable by Article 3(g) of the Statute of the Tribunal; and COUNT 14: CRIMES AGAINST HUMANITY,(other inhumane acts), punishable by Article 3(i) of the Statute of the Tribunal; and

COUNT 15: VIOLATIONS OF ARTICLE 3 COMMON TO THE GENEVA CONVENTIONS AND OF ARTICLE 4(2)(e) OF ADDITIONAL PROTOCOL 2, as incorporated by Article 4(e)(outrages upon personal dignity, in particular rape, degrading and humiliating treatment and indecent assault) of the Statute of the Tribunal.

DATE: 17 June 1997

Louise Arbour
Prosecutor

Bibliography

Abbreviations

AFP	Agence France Presse
AN	Africa News
AP	Associated Press
APW	AP Worldstream
BBC	British Broadcasting Corporation
DPI	Department of Public Information (UN)
EIU	Economist Intelligence Unit
ICG	International Crisis Group
NYT	New York Times

AAP Newsfeed (1998), '35 Get Life Sentence for Rwanda Genocide,' 7 June, *available in* Lexis, News Library.

Africa News (1999a), 'Three Judges Sworn in at ICTR,' 22 Feb., *available in* Lexis, News Library.

Africa News (1999b), 'Rwanda: Tribunal Update,' 28 April, *available in* Lexis, News Library.

Africa News (1999c), 'Former Rwandan Mayor Gets Life in Swiss Trial,' 3 May, *available in* Lexis, News Library.

African Rights (1995a), *Rwanda: Death, Despair, and Defiance*. London.

African Rights (1995b), *Rwanda: Not so Innocent: When Women Become Killers*. London.

Agence France Presse (1995), 'Kenyan Will Not Protect Rwandan Killers: Moi,' 10 Oct., *available in* Lexis, News Library.

Agence France Presse (1996a), 'Ethiopia Extradites Genocide suspect,' 22 July, *available in* Lexis, News Library.

Agence France Presse (1996b), '365 People Killed in Rwanda: UN,' 22 Aug., *available in* Lexis, News Library.

Agence France Presse (1997a), 'Rwandans to Swap Notes with S. African Truth Body on War Crimes,' 17 Jan., *available in* Lexis, News Library.
Agence France Presse (1997b), 'Burundian Sentenced to Death in Rwandan War Crimes Trial,' 21 Jan., *available in* Lexis, News Library.
Agence France Presse (1997c), 'Gang-rape in Rwanda Was to Humiliate Us: Witness,' 24 Oct., *available in* Lexis, News Library.
Agence France Presse (1997d), 24 Oct., 'Mayor Encouraged Rapists like Players, Rwanda Court Told,' 24 Oct., *available in* Lexis, News Library.
Agence France Presse (1999), 'Rwandan Courts Tried 864 Genocide Suspects Last Year: Official,' 19 Jan., *available in* Lexis, News Library.
André, Catherine and Jean-Philippe Platteau (1998), 'Land Relations under Unbearable Stress: Rwanda Caught in the Malthusian Trap,' *Journal of Economic Behavior and Organization,* vol. 34, pp. 1-47.
AP Worldstream (1998a), 'Critical Swedish Judge to Step Down from Rwanda Tribunal,' 18 July, *available in* Lexis, News Library.
AP Worldstream, (1998b), 'Rwanda Tribunal Registrar Rejects Charges of Mismanagement,' 23 July, *available in* Lexis, News Library.
Associated Press (1995), 'Rwanda War Crimes Tribunal Holds First Session,' 29 June, *available in* Lexis, News Library.
Associated Press (1998), 'UN, U.S. blamed for Failure to Stop Rwandan Genocide,' *Gazette* (Montreal), 16 Dec., *available in* Lexis, News Library.
Austin, G. (1996), *The Effects of Government Policy on the Ethnic Distribution of Income and Wealth in Rwanda: A Review of Published Sources*, Consultancy Report for the World Bank, Washington, DC.
Bassiouni, M. Cherif (1995), 'Former Yugoslavia: Investigating Violations of International Humanitarian Law and Establishing an International Criminal Tribunal,' *Fordham International Law Review,* vol. 18, pp. 1191-1210.
Berkeley, Bill (1998), 'Judgement Day,' *Washington Post*, 11 Oct., p. W10.
Blanchfield, Mike (1998a), 'General Battles Rwanda "Demons": After Witnessing the Atrocities of Genocide, Romeo Dallaire Has Had to Endure the Belgian Government's Criticism,' *Ottawa Cirizen*, 13 Dec., p. A3, *available in* Lexis, News Library.
Blanchfield, Mike (1998b), 'Reliving a Tutsi Woman's Terror,' *Ottawa Citizen*, 22 Feb., p. A10, *available in* Lexis, News Library.
Bonner, Raymond (1994), 'Rwanda's Leaders Vow to Build a Multiparty State for both Hutu and Tutsi,' *New York Times*, 7 Sept., p. A10, *available in* Lexis, News Library.
British Broadcasting Corp. (1996), 'Notorious Genocide Suspect Arrives from Ethiopia,' 16 Sept., *available in* Lexis, News Library.

British Broadcasting Corp. (1997), 'Government Statement on International Tribunal in Arusha,' Radio Rwanda, Kigali, 25 Feb., *available in* Lexis, News Library.
Burkhalter, Holly (1994), 'Ending the Cycle of Retribution in Rwanda,' *Legal Times*, 22 Aug., p.19.
Chrétien, Jean-Pierre (1995), *Rwanda: Les Médias du Génocide*. Paris, Karthala.
Codere, Helen (1962), 'Power in Rwanda,' *Anthropologica*, vol. 4, pp. 45-85.
Crossette, Barbara (1995), 'War Crimes Judge Says Rwanda Probes Being Hampered,' *International Herald Tribune*, 30 Dec., *available in* Lexis, News Library.
Department of Public Information (1996), *The United Nations and Rwanda*, 1993-1996, UN Blue Book Series, vol. X, New York.
Des Forges, Alison (1999), *Leave None to Tell the Story: Genocide in Rwanda*, London, Human Rights Watch.
Destexhe, Alain (1995), *Rwanda and Genocide in the Twentieth Century*, New York, New York University Press.
Economist Intelligence Unit (1983a), *Rwanda Country Report* No. 4.
Economist Intelligence Unit (1983b), *Rwanda Country Report*. Annual supplement.
Economist Intelligence Unit (1993), *Rwanda Country Report* No. 1.
Eriksson, John (1996), *The International Response to Conflict and Genocide: Lessons from the Rwanda Experience: Synthesis Report of the Joint Evaluation of Emergency Assistance to Rwanda*, Copenhagen.
Fox, David (1997), 'Lawyers' Group Readies for Rwanda Genocide Appeal,' *Reuters World Service*, 7 Jan., *available in* Lexis, News Library.
Goldstone, Richard (1995), 'Statement by Justice Richard Goldstone,' ICTR, 5 Oct., The Hague.
Gourevitch, Philip (1998a), *We Wish to Inform You That Tomorrow We Will Be Killed with Our Families*, New York, Farrar Straus and Giroux.
Gourevitch, Philip (1998b), 'The Genocide Fax,' *New Yorker*, 11 May.
Grogan, Ewart and Arthur Sharp (1900), *From the Cape to Cairo: the First Traverse of Africa South to North*, London, Hurst and Blackett.
Hardy, Paul (1999), 'The Man Who Chose to Act for Genocide Defendants,' *The Times* (London), 9 March, *available in* Lexis, News Library.
Hilsum, Lindsey (1995), 'Rwanda Justice Grinds to a Halt,' *The Observer*, 12 Nov., p. 25, *available in* Lexis, News Library.
Hilsum, Lindsey (1997), 'UN Tribunal Hears the Horror of Tutsis' Massacre in Rwanda,' *Sacramento Bee*, 23 Jan., p. B7, *available in* Lexis, News Library.

Hirondelle (1998a), 'ICTR/Kambanda: Former Prime Minister Files an Appeal against His Life Sentence,' 7 Sept. (available at www.hirondelle.org).

Hirondelle (1998b), 'ICTR/Kambanda: Former Rwandan Prime Minister Sentenced to Life for Genocide Insists upon the Lawyer of His Choice,' 14 Oct. (available at www.hirondelle.org).

Igwara, Obi (1995), 'Ethnicity, Nationalism and Genocide in Rwanda,' In O. Igwara (ed.) *Ethnic Hatred: Genocide in Rwanda*. London: ASEN. pp. 1-18.

International Crisis Group, (1999), *Report: Five Years after the Genocide in Rwanda:Justice in Question*, 7 April, Brussels (available at www.crisisweb.org).

Jefremovas, Villia (1995), 'Acts of Human Kindness: Tutsi, Hutu, and the Genocide,' *Issue,* vol. 23, no. 2, pp. 28-31.

Jones, John R. (1998), *The Practice of the International Criminal Tribunals for the Former Yugoslavia and Rwanda*, New York, Transnational Publishers.

Kaban, Elif (1995), 'Rwanda Pledges to Do More to Heal Ethnic Rifts,' *Reuters*, 2 Nov., *available in* Lexis, News Library.

Kaban, Elif (1996), 'Rwanda Seeks Ethiopian-detained Genocide Suspect,' *Reuters World Service*, 14 June, *available in* Lexis, News Library.

Kamukama, Dixon (1997), *Rwanda Conflict: Its Roots and Regional Implications*, Kampala, Uganda, Fountain Press.

Karnavas, Michael G. (1997), 'Rwanda's Quest for Justice: National and International Efforts and Challenges,' *The Champion*, pp. 16-19, 57-60, May.

Kibanga, Premy (1997), 'Separate Rwanda, Bosnia Tribunals, Urges Kigali Govt,' *East African*, 3-9 March, p. 4.

Kotch, Nicholas (1997), 'Rwanda's Genocide Law Defines Guilt and Punishment,' *Reuters World Service*, 25 Sept., *available in* Lexis, News Library.

Lemarchand, René (1970), *Rwanda and Burundi*, London, Pall Mall.

Lemarchand, René (1995), 'Rwanda: The Rationality of Genocide,' *Issue*, vol. 23, no. 2, pp. 8-11.

Lemarchand, René (1996), *Burundi: Ethnic Conflict and Genocide*, Cambridge, Cambridge University Press.

Lorch, Donatella (1995), 'Kenya Refuses to Hand Over Suspects in Rwanda Slayings,' *New York Times*, 6 Oct., p. A3.

Louis, Wm. Rogers (1963), *Ruanda-Urundi, 1884-1919*, Oxford, Clarendon Press.

Lupis, Ingrid Detter de (1987), *The Law of War*, New York, Columbia University Press.

Macintosh, Anne (1995), 'The International Response: Escape from Genocide,' In O. Igwara (ed.) *Ethnic Hatred: Genocide in Rwanda*. London: ASEN. pp. 73-83.

Magnarella, Paul J. (1993), *Human Materialism: A Model of Sociocultural Systems and a Strategy for Analysis*, Gainesville, FL., University Press of Florida.

Magnarella, Paul J. (1995), 'Trying for Peace through Law: The UN Tribunal for the Former Yugoslavia,' *Human Peace*, vol. 10, pp. 3-8.

Magnarella, Paul J. (1998), 'The U.S. Can Extradite Fugitives to the UN Criminal Tribunals,' *American Society of International Law Human Rights Newsletter,* vol. 8, no. 3.

Maquet, J.J. (1954, 'The Kingdom of Ruanda,' in D. Forde (ed.), *African Worlds*, London, Oxford University Press, pp. 164-189.

Maquet, J.J. (1961), *The Premise of Inequality in Ruanda*, London, Oxford University Press.

Marie, Alphonse (1995), 'Statement by the Minister of Justice of Rwanda to the First Public Hearing of the First Session of the International Criminal Tribunal for Rwanda,' The Hague, 27 June.

Maton, J. (1994), 'Développement économique et social au Rwanda entre 1980 et 1993. Le dixiéme décile en face de l'apocalypse,' Department of Economics (University of Gent Belgium).

Mbanda, Laurent (1997), *Committed to Conflict*, London, SPCK.

McCoubrey, Hilaire (1990), *International Humanitarian Law*, Brookfield, VT, Gower.

McKinley, James C. (1998), 'Ex-Premier Admits He Led Massacres in Rwanda in 1994,' *New York Times*, 2 May, p. A1, *available in* Lexis, News Library.

Mecklenburg, Frederick, Duke of. (1910), *In the Heart of Africa*, London, Cassel.

Megreal, Chris (1997), 'Survivors Confront Rwandan Butcher,' *Guardian* (London), 16 Jan., p. 13, *available in* Lexis, News Library.

Megreal, Chris (1998), 'From Reluctant Premier to Mass Murderer,' *Observer* (Ottowa), 6 Sept., *available in* Lexis, News Library.

Meron, Theodor (1994), 'War Crimes in Yugoslavia and Development of International Law,' *American Journal of International Law*, vol. 88, pp. 78-87.

Monitor (1998), 'Fresh Trouble as Judge Curses Rwanda Tribunal,' Africa News Online, May 2.

Morris, Madeline H. (1997), 'The Trials of Concurrent Jurisdiction: The Case of Rwanda,' *Duke Journal of Comparative and International Law*, vol. 7, pp. 349-374.

Morris, V.A. & M.P. Scharf (1998), *The International Criminal Tribunal for Rwanda*, Vol. 1-2, New York, Transnational Publishers.

Newbury, Catharine (1988), *The Cohesion of Oppression*, New York, Columbia University Press.

Newbury, Catharine (1995), 'Background to Genocide in Rwanda,' *Issue*, vol. 23, no. 2, pp. 12-17.

New York Times (1997), 'Rwanda to Execute 2 Hutu; First Verdict on '94 Killings,' 3 Jan., *available in* Lexis, News Library.

Noubissie, Emmanuel (1996), 'Cameroon Snubs Rwanda Genocide Tribunal Official,' *Reuters*, 2 Oct., *available in* Lexis, News Library.

Nyankanzi, Edward L. (1998), *Genocide: Rwanda and Burundi*, Rochester, VT, Schenkman.

Okali, Agwu (1998), 'Peace with Justice: The Contribution of the International Criminal Tribunal for Rwanda,' Address at UN International School Student Conference, 6 March, New York.

Oppenheim, Lassa (1952), *International Law, A Treatise. Disputes, War and Neutrality*, 7th ed., Hersch Lauterpacht (ed.), Longman, Green, London.

Ottawa Citizen (1998), 'Annan Blames UN Members for Slaughter in Rwanda,' 5 May, p. A7, *available in* Lexis, News Library.

Pottier, Johan (1995), 'Representations of Ethnicity in Post-Genocide Writings on Rwanda,' In O. Igwara (ed.) *Ethnic Hatred: Genocide in Rwanda*, London, ASEN, pp. 35-58.

Preston, Julia (1994), 'Tribunal Set on Rwanda War Crimes; Kigali Votes No on UN Resolution,' *Washington Post*, Nov. 9, p. A44.

Prosecutor versus Jean-Paul Akayesu (1998), International Criminal Tribunal for Rwanda, Case No. ICTR-96-4-T, Judgment, 2 September .

Prosecutor vs. Jean Kambanda (1998), Case No. ICTR 97-23-S, Judgment and Sentence, 4 Sept.

Prunier, Gerard (1997), *The Rwanda Crisis*, London, Hurst and Co.

Santoro, Lara (1998), 'Rwanda Massacres Were Avoidable, General Says,' *Christian Science Monitor*, 27 Feb., p. 7, *available in* Lexis, News Library.

Reuters (1995), 'Rwanda Conference Recommends Genocide Courts,' 24 Jan., *available in* Lexis, News Library.

Reuters (1997), 'UN Rwanda Genocide Tribunal Receives Key Accused,' 24 Jan., *available in* Lexis, News Library.

Schabas, William A. (1996), 'Prosecuting International Crime: Justice, Democracy, and Impunity in Post-Genocide Rwanda: Searching for Solutions to Impossible Problems,' *Criminal Law Forum*, vol. 7, pp. 523-559.

Schabas, William A. (1997), 'Rwanda Should Abandon Use of Death Penalty,' *Gazette* (Montreal), 19 Feb., p. B3.

Scharf, Michael P. (1997), *Balkan Justice*, Durham, NC, Carolina Academic Press.

Seavoy, Ronald E. (1989), *Famine in East Africa: Food Production and Food Policies*, New York, Greenwood.

Sellstrom, Tor and Wohlgemuth, Lennart (1996), *The International Response to Conflict and Genocide: Lessons from the Rwanda Experience: Historical Perspective: Some Explanatory Factors*, Joint Evaluation of Emergency Assistance to Rwanda, Copenhagen.

Tadesse, Tsegaye (1996), 'Ethiopia to Deport Rwandan Genocide Suspect,' Reuters World Service, 14 June, *available in* Lexis, News Library.

Thomas, Anni (1994), 'Rwandan Government Promises to Work with War Crimes Court,' *Agence France Presse*, 24 Nov., *available in* Lexis, News Library.

Thompson, Allan (1998), 'We're All Guilty in Killings, Dallaire Blames World's Inaction in Rwanda,' *Toronto Star*, 26 Feb., *available in* Lexis, News Library.

Toronto Star (1998), 'French General Takes Aim at Dallaire,' 20 May, *available in* Lexis, News Library.

Tunbridge, Louis (1995), 'Kenya Sheltering Suspects in Rwandan Atrocities,' *Daily Telegraph*, 3 Nov., p. 20, *available in* Lexis, News Library.

Ubutabera (1998) 'The Akayesu Case,' No. 31, 2 March (Independent Newsletter of the ICTR).

Van Lierop, Robert F. (1997) 'Rwanda Evaluation: Report and Recommendations,' *Tort and Insurance Law Journal*, vol. 31, pp. 887-903.

Vassall-Adams, Guy (1994), *Rwanda*, Oxford, Oxfam.

Wedgwood, Ruth (1994), 'War Crimes in the Former Yugoslavia: Comments on the International War Crimes Tribunal,' *Virginia Journal of International Law*, Vol. 34, pp. 267-275.

Zarembo, Alan (1998) 'The Execution of Justice,' *Newsweek*, 11 May, p. 21, *available in* Lexis, News Library.

Index

Adede, Andronido 44, 53, 61, 63
Akayesu, Jean-Paul 54, 95-96, 99-110, 112
Albright, U.S. Secretary of State Madeleine 32
Amegadjie, Georges Komlave 67
Amnesty International 78
Annan, Kofi 32, 60, 63, 106-107
Arbour, Louise 44, 54, 64, 69, 100
Arusha Accords 16-17, 18, 19, 22, 30, 31, 41, 59, 72
Aspegren, Judge Lennart 65-66, 87, 97
Atita, Paul Kato 79
Avocats sans Frontiéres (Lawyers without Borders) 76-77

Bagosora, Theoneste 53-54, 86
Bizimungu, Pasteur 22, 42, 78
Boutros-Ghali, Boutros 32
Burundi 10, 17-18, 20, 47

Clinton, U.S. President Bill 32
Coalition pour la Défense de la République (CDR) 16
colonial rule
 Belgium 10-12
 German 9-10
corvée labor 5, 11
crimes against humanity
 defined 46-47, 100-103

Dallaire, General Romeo 31-36, 106-107
Degni-Ségui, René, Special Rapporteur on Human Rights 37
Democratic Republican Movement 77, 85, 95
Des Forges, Alison 105
diet 5, 7, 22-25, 27

economy
 coffee exports 25
 food production 22-25
 generally 22-27
 tourism 25
 tin mining 25
ethnic identity cards 11-12, 15, 98
ethnic quota policy 14, 15

famine 11
Flamme, Jean 76
Fondation Hirondelle 55, 69n, 84n, 110n
Forces Armées Rwandaises (FAR) 19, 21, 25, 30, 35, 36, 88
foreign aid 29, 75, 77, 111
FRODEBU (*Front pour la democracy au Burundi*) 18

Gahima, Gerard, Rwandan Deputy Justice Minister 78

Geneva Conventions
  Common Article 3 45-48, 111
  Additional Protocol II 45-48, 111
genocide
  causes of 22-27
  defined 46, 87, 97-99
Goldstone, Richard 44, 51, 96, 100

Habyarimana, Juvénal 14-19, 22, 24-26, 31-33, 36, 51, 85-86, 88
Hamitic Myth 10
Hilsum, Lindsey 105
human materialism: an explanatory paradigm 1-2, 24
Hutu
  defined 3
Hutu Manifesto 12, 13
Hutu Power 17, 32

Impuzamugambi ('Those with a single purpose') 18, 24
Inglis, Michael Oliver 91, 92
Interahamwe ('Those who attack together') 18, 20, 25, 31, 88, 93, 106
intermarriage 6, 14-15
Intermédia 55
International Committee of the Red Cross (ICRC) 71
International Criminal Tribunal for Rwanda (ICTR)
  appellate judges 44
  budgets 57n
  composition of the tribunal 44
  creating the tribunal 42-43
  first trials 34, 85-93, 95-110
  indictments 50-53
  jurisdiction
    concurrent 48-49
    personal 44-45, 83-84
    subject matter 45-48
  rules of procedure 49-50
  trial judges 44, 51
  tribunal primacy 48-49

International Criminal Tribunal for the Former Yugoslavia (ICTY) 43, 59

Kabiligi, Colonel Gratien 86
Kagame, Paul 22, 64
Kama, Judge Laity 44, 66, 67, 87, 97, 107
Kambanda, Jean 54-55, 63, 65, 85-93, 112
Kangura 16, 19
Karamira, Froduald 77-80
Karnavus, Michael G. 65, 96
Kayibanda, Gregoire 13, 14, 85
Kigri V, King 13
Kinyarwanda 3, 44, 98
Kwihutura 4

Ligue Rwandaise pour la Promotion et la Défense des Droits de l'Homme (Rwandan League for the Promotion and Defense of Human Rights) 81

Matata, Joseph 106
Mitterrand, French President François 15, 35, 36
Moghalu, Kingsley 69
Moi, Kenyan President Daniel arap 51, 86
Mouvement Révolutionnaire National pour le Développement (MRND) 14, 17, 76
Muna, Bernard Acho 63, 65, 68, 91, 92
Musema, Alfred 55
Museveni, Yoweri 15, 19
Musinga, King Yuhi 10
Mwinyi, Ali Hassan 19

Nahimana, Ferinand 54
Naki (Nairobi-Kigali plan) 86
Ndadaye, Melchior 18
Ngeze, Hassan 16, 86

Nitonteze, Fulgence 93
Nsabimana, Sylvain 86
Nsengiyumva, Colonel Anatole 54
Ntabakuze, Commander Aloys 86
Ntagerura, André 54
Ntahobali, Arsene Shalom 86
Ntahobali, Pauline, Minister of Family and Social Welfare 86, 87
Ntuyahaga, Bernard 66-69
Nuremberg Charter 45-48

Obote, Milton 15
Okali, Agwu Ukiwe 59, 63, 64, 65-66, 68, 69
Operation Turquoise 35-36
Organic Law of Rwanda 73-74
Organization of African Unity (OAU) 16, 30, 31, 35
Ostrosky, Judge Yakov 44, 67, 87

PARMEHUTU 13
Paschke, Karl 60
Paschke Report I 60-63
Paschke Report II 65
Pillay, Judge Navanethem 44, 51, 87, 97
population 2, 24, 27, 29
Presidential Guard 19, 20, 36
Programme de Suivi des Accusés de Génocide mis en liberté (PSAG) 81-83
Prosecutor v. Akayesu 19, 39, 54, 95-110, 112
Prosecutor v. Kambanda 54, 85-93, 112

Quesnot, General Christian 36, 38

Radio Milles Collines 17, 21, 54, 88
Rakotomanana, Honore 44, 62, 63
rape
  as crime against humanity and genocide 100-103

Refugee Crisis 36-37, 74
religion 7-8, 26
Riza, Iqbal 32
Rutaganda, Georges 55
Ruzindana, Mathias 105
Ruzindana, Obed 55
Rwanda
  criticism of ICTR 55, 62-64
  genocide courts 73-74, 75-76
  geography 2
  independence 12-13
  justice system 71-74, 75-77
  military justice 83-84
  pre-colonial culture 6-8
  pre-colonial history 3-7
  Second Republic 14-19
Rwabugiri, King Kegeri 3
Rwandan Popular Front (RPF) 15, 17, 21, 22, 25, 35, 36, 41, 59, 71, 83, 86
Rwigema, Pierre Claver 22

Scheers, Johan 92, 96
Serushago, Omar 54
Sexual violence
  as crime against humanity and genocide 100-103
Shattuck, John, U.S. Assistant Secretary of State for Human Rights 41
Sindikubwabo, Theodore 86, 88

Temmerman, Luc de 96
Ten Commandments of the Hutu 16
Tiangaye, Nicolas 96, 108
Tutsi
  defined 3
Twa
  defined 3
Twagiramungu, Faustin 22

Ubuhake 7
Uburetwa 5

United Nations
    UN Assistance Mission for
        Rwanda (UNAMIR) 31-36,
        62, 106
    UN Independent Inquiry 27, 39

UN Security Council 22, 42, 43,
    48, 59, 112
UNAMIR II 36
Uwilingiyimana, Prime Minister
    Agathe 34, 67, 86